T0334075

Cambridge Elements ≡

Elements in Psycholinguistics
edited by
Paul Warren
Victoria University of Wellington

VERBAL IRONY PROCESSING

Stephen Skalicky
Victoria University of Wellington

CAMBRIDGE
UNIVERSITY PRESS

Shaftesbury Road, Cambridge CB2 8EA, United Kingdom

One Liberty Plaza, 20th Floor, New York, NY 10006, USA

477 Williamstown Road, Port Melbourne, VIC 3207, Australia

314–321, 3rd Floor, Plot 3, Splendor Forum, Jasola District Centre,
New Delhi – 110025, India

103 Penang Road, #05–06/07, Visioncrest Commercial, Singapore 238467

Cambridge University Press is part of Cambridge University Press & Assessment,
a department of the University of Cambridge.

We share the University's mission to contribute to society through the pursuit of
education, learning and research at the highest international levels of excellence.

www.cambridge.org
Information on this title: www.cambridge.org/9781009234542

DOI: 10.1017/9781009234566

First published 2023

A catalogue record for this publication is available from the British Library.

ISBN 978-1-009-23454-2 Paperback
ISSN 2753-9768 (online)
ISSN 2753-975X (print)

Verbal Irony Processing

Elements in Psycholinguistics

DOI: 10.1017/9781009234566
First published online: January 2023

Stephen Skalicky
Victoria University of Wellington
Author for correspondence: Stephen Skalicky, stephen.skalicky@vuw.ac.nz

Abstract: Ironic language is a salient reminder that speakers of all languages do not always mean what they say. While ironic language has captured the attention of theorists and scholars for centuries, it is only since the 1980s that psycholinguistic methods have been employed to investigate how readers and hearers detect, process, and comprehend ironic language. This Element reviews the foundational definitions, theories, and psycholinguistic models of ironic language, covering key questions such as the distinction between literal and ironic meaning, the role of contextual information during irony processing, and the cognitive mechanisms involved. These key questions continue to motivate new studies and methodological innovations, providing ample opportunity for future researchers who wish to continue exploring how ironic language is processed and understood.

Keywords: verbal irony, sarcasm, pragmatics, figurative language, psycholinguistics

ISBNs: 9781009234542 (PB), 9781009234566 (OC)
ISSNs: 2753-9768 (online), 2753-975X (print)

Contents

1 Introduction: Is It Ironic?

In 1995, Canadian singer Alanis Morissette released the album *Jagged Little Pill*. Among the tracks on the album was a song titled *Ironic*, in which the lyrics recounted a series of events such as rain occurring on a wedding day, an elderly person winning the lottery and then dying, or being stuck in traffic when one was already late. The song's refrain (*And isn't it ironic . . . don't you think?*) has been vociferously answered by many a listener with a resounding *no!* over the years since the song's release. The reason for this response was that many listeners and critics felt that some or all of the situations depicted in the song were not actually ironic. Instead, they felt these situations would be better described as coincidental or simply unfortunate. Taking the criticism in stride, Morissette has publicly admitted that she and her producer did not carefully check whether each and every example in the song conformed to the definition of irony, resulting in an unfortunate irony that a song about irony did not actually contain examples of irony. In 2015, Morissette appeared on *The Late Late Show with James Corden* in the USA and performed an updated version of *Ironic* with lyrics taking into account updates in technology and social media since 1995. One line from the new rendition, "It's liking singing *Ironic*, when there are no ironies," further spoke to Morissette's admission that the original version of the song included examples of nonironic situations.

As such, the debate over the examples in *Ironic* has become seemingly as well known as the song itself. Indeed, on the *Wikipedia* entry for *Ironic*, the first main section of the entry contains a subsection titled *linguistic dispute*, which summarizes the debate regarding the song's examples and doubles down on the claim that some examples in the song are not actually ironic (Wikipedia, 2022). The rationale used by the author(s) of the *Wikipedia* article is that some of the examples in the song do not adhere to the definition of irony as provided by the *Oxford English Dictionary* (OED). The definition cited from the OED is as follows: "A state of affairs or an event that seems deliberately contrary to what was or might be expected; an outcome cruelly, humorously, or strangely at odds with assumptions or expectations" (Oxford English Dictionary, 2022).

Others have come to Morissette's defense, claiming that the lyrics of *Ironic* depict ironic events. In a 2014 article published by the online magazine *Salon*, author Michael Reid Roberts pointed to the same OED definition cited by *Wikipedia* to argue that each of the situations described in the song were indeed ironic because the examples used in the song are all examples of what is known as situational irony (Roberts, 2014). Roberts further drew from literary sources to emphasize that there are many different types of irony, and that each example in *Ironic* can be assigned to one of these types of irony.

So, who is right? Are the legions of comedians, talk show hosts, and layperson critics who have lambasted Morissette for misuse of the term wrong? Is the OED definition of irony deficit in its ability to categorize events as ironic or nonironic? Does the OED even possess the authority to put forth a definition of irony for which examples can be judged? And what about the range of literary definitions Roberts (2014) draws from – are they wrong?

It turns out that the public debate over Morissette's use of the term *ironic* bears a similarity to the academic scholarship surrounding irony. In particular, arriving at a precise definition of irony has sparked a considerable amount of academic debate across disciplinary boundaries. And, intertwined with that debate rests the psycholinguistic research which has sought to uncover how people process and comprehend ironic meaning. Over the past decades, a combination of pragmatic theory and empirical investigation via psycholinguistic methods has provided insight into the nature of irony. However, unlike the Morissette song, most of this research has been focused specifically on ironic language – verbal irony.

It is necessary at this point to clarify the distinction between *verbal* irony and *situational* irony. The song *Ironic* includes examples of situational irony, depicting events or contexts which defy the expectations of those experiencing the event, typically to the experiencers' detriment (Lucariello, 1994; Shelley, 2001). Verbal irony instead refers to ironic communication, whether that be in speech or writing, and may also manifest as sarcasm, hyperbole, ironic praise, ironic criticism, and more (Colston, 2017). However, the distinction between situational and verbal irony is mostly a matter of framing. With a few adjustments, all of the ironic situations in *Ironic* could garner ironic statements *about* the situation depicted in the song: *What lovely weather for a wedding* (It's like rain on your wedding day); *He sure is lucky!* (Dying a day after winning the lottery), and so on. As will become evident throughout this Element, irony (whether verbal or situational) relies on a contrast between situation and expectations. That being said, the bulk of psycholinguistic research has focused primarily on verbal irony, and thus all subsequent mentions of irony in this Element will refer to verbal irony.

1.1 What Is Verbal Irony?

Pretend you are watching a movie in a theater with one of your close friends. While watching the movie, an audience member in front of you begins using their smartphone to send text messages and check their social media accounts. The brightness of their phone screen and noise from the audio notifications is causing a distraction, and many people are casting dirty looks toward the phone user. Becoming annoyed, your friend leans toward you and says: "I sure love it when people turn off their phones during a movie!"

How would you interpret the meaning of your friend's utterance? On the surface, the friend's statement adheres with the syntactic constraints of the English language and is semantically acceptable. There is also little reason to think your friend is telling a lie or does not truly believe the statement which they have just uttered. Yet, something about this statement implies your friend might be hinting at some other meaning beyond what they have said. In order to figure out what your friend might truly mean, there are a number of other factors which you may consider. The first is the contrast between the context- ual situation and your friend's utterance – why would your friend state their preference for silenced phones when another patron was so obviously violat- ing that preference? To answer this question, you might try to emulate your friend's perspective or point of view – asking yourself why they would make a statement to inform you of their preference in the first place. Your analysis might suggest that your friend is attempting to convey not only semantic but also pragmatic or attitudinal meaning. You might also notice something about the way your friend spoke the utterance – did they use a particular tone of voice or emphasize certain words? You then might also consider what you know about your friend – their personality, their occupation, and the rate they normally use sarcasm. Crucially, you would likely complete your assessment of this situation almost automatically, without exerting conscious control over the integration of the linguistic, pragmatic, and contextual information avail- able. Your final consideration of some or all of these factors (and potentially others) may then lead you to the conclusion that your friend is being ironic, specifically as a means to make clear their disapproval for the other person's use of a cell phone during a movie.

As it turns out, your fictional friend is employing verbal irony. Many explanations of verbal irony rely upon an oppositional contrast between what is said and what is meant, usually to the extent that a speaker is thought to *not* agree with what they are stating (e.g., exclaiming *what lovely weather* during a hailstorm). This oppositional clash can be positive, such as when a seemingly negative comment is made to provide a compliment or positive assessment (e.g., one person stating to their friend *you are so selfish* after learning their friend volunteers at an animal shelter). Perhaps more prototypically, verbal irony can be negative, such as when a seemingly positive comment is made as a means to provide criticism, commonly referred to a sarcasm (e.g., a disgruntled airline passenger stating *what great service!* after finding that their luggage has been lost). However, not all examples of verbal irony need demonstrate a clearly oppositional contrast, which is why I have specifically chosen to use the aforementioned cell phone example as a means to foreground the contrast between what is said and aspects of the surrounding context. Surely, your fictional friend prefers for people to *not* use their cell phone during a movie, and by stating this preference in light of a clear violation of this preference, a tension between what is said and *what is occurring* becomes salient. The true meaning of your friend's utterance then takes on a range of possibilities, most of which hinge upon a clear disapproval for the actions of the cell phone using patron.

Because verbal irony triggers a contrast between what is said and what is meant, verbal irony can be defined as a type of *figurative language*. At its core, figurative language is " . . . speech where speakers mean something other than what they say" (Gibbs & Colston, 2012, p. 1). As such, verbal irony is in the company of other types of figurative language such as metaphor, metonymy, idioms, proverbs, and more. In all instances of figurative language, there is some degree of departure between the surface level meaning of an utterance and the actual intended (figurative) meaning of the speaker. Many psycholinguistic (and other) studies of figurative language tend to describe this difference as a contrast between the *literal* and *figurative* meanings of an utterance. Yet, as pointed out by Gibbs and Colston (2012), this definition of figurative language quickly collapses under scrutiny. Other types of nonfigurative language (including so-called literal language) also involve departures between what is said and what is meant, and as such trying to distinguish the figurative from the nonfigurative may ultimately be futile (Gibbs & Colston, 2012). Instead, it may be more fruitful to investigate the specific ways people create and resolve the difference between what is said and what is meant for specific types of (figurative) language.

As will be argued, verbal irony tends to include some sort of contradiction between the *situation* and an utterance as a means to guide the hearer toward resolving the difference between what is said and what is meant. The exact mechanisms behind this process are what have attracted particular attention from psycholinguistics. However, explanations of verbal irony processing and comprehension emerged initially from pragmatics, likely because ironic meaning is largely a pragmatic phenomenon. As such, in order to understand the psycholinguistic research into verbal irony processing, it is necessary to first review the pragmatic definitions of verbal irony because they have left an indelible mark on the field.

1.2 The Standard Pragmatic Model of Verbal Irony

Early theoretical models of verbal irony suggested that the figurative meaning of an ironic utterance is the direct opposite of what was said. The rationale for this view is drawn from what is now referred to as the *standard pragmatic model* (SPM). The core arguments of the SPM can be found in Grice's work on conversational implicature (Grice, 1975, 1978, 1989), in which a distinction is made between what is said and what is meant. From this view, a hearer will consider first the surface level meaning of an utterance, assess that meaning against norms of conversation (such as Gricean maxims of conversation), and only then integrate pragmatic knowledge in order to fully understand what is meant (in this case, irony). Because Grice described the intended meaning of irony to be the negation or the reverse of what was said, the SPM would thus predict that when a listener encounters an ironic phrase, the listener must first interpret the literal meaning of an utterance, reject the meaning, and then consider the opposite meaning to be the ironic meaning (Gibbs, 1986b; Giora, 2003; Wilson & Sperber, 1992).

The definition of ironic meaning put forth by Grice was unable to withstand a number of subsequent theoretical arguments and empirical evidence from research studies. One of the main reasons for an initial rejection of the Gricean definition was that many examples of nonoppositional irony could be invented or had been observed. For example, consider the fictional friend's utterance – the opposite meaning would be something approximate to the friend stating that they do *not* enjoy it when people turn off their smartphones during a movie. However, all evidence would suggest otherwise (i.e., the friend clearly *does* prefer for phones to be off), and thus the ironic meaning behind the friend's utterance is something else. Clearly then, a definition of irony had to be more than the opposite of the surface, literal meaning. As such, a lineage of verbal irony definitions has been offered as a means to explain the full range of ironic expressions. Looking back from the present, these subsequent definitions of verbal irony all shared the same goal of producing the most parsimonious definition which could account for all instances and types of verbal irony. A good overview of many of these theories can be found in Gibbs and Colston (2007), which contains a discussion of the theories as well as reprints of the original articles associated with the theories. What follows is a brief summary of some of these theories and models.

1.3 Reactions to the SPM: Broadening the Definition of Verbal Irony

One early alternative to the SPM drew from relevance theory to describe the relationship between an ironic utterance and its meaning as one of *use-mention*

(Sperber & Wilson, 1981; Wilson & Sperber, 1992). From this point of view, an ironic utterance *echoes* or reflects some specific utterance or an implicit belief while also channeling a disapproving attitude. Applied to the movie example, the friend's utterance could be said to echo the implicit belief held in many cultures that movie theater patrons should not use cell phones during a movie. The echoic view of irony thus applies to a larger number of ironic utterances, such as those which are more than stating the opposite of what one believes. The use-mention theory was also more flexible because the ironic echo can refer to almost any sort of preexisting belief or value, implied or explicit.

A number of additional pragmatic models of verbal irony have since been put forth. The *pretense* view of irony claimed to be able to explain an even wider number of examples. From this view, an ironic speaker takes on the role of a naïve commentator as a means to signal their true ironic intentions (Clark & Gerrig, 1984). A subsequent view, called the *allusional pretense theory*, argued that the range of ironic examples covered by the use-mention and pretense theories could all be explained by describing irony as a combination of being insincere while alluding to failed expectations, which in turn expresses the speaker's attitude toward the violation (Kumon-Nakamura et al., 1995). A later view described verbal irony as *relevant inappropriateness* (Attardo, 2000). As the name suggests, Attardo claimed that verbal irony can be explained as an utterance that is relevant yet also inappropriate in a particular context. From this view, the test for whether some utterance is inappropriate or not is based on contextual factors. Finally, a later conceptualization of verbal irony put forth the idea that verbal irony is fundamentally a *clash* between what is said and what the speaker intends to communicate (Garmendia, 2014). Garmendia (2014) argued that all examples of verbal irony contain such a clash and thus this description was more encompassing than the prior theories covered in this section.

1.4 A Parsimonious Definition of Verbal Irony

The review in Section 1.3 is merely a glimpse yet should make clear a general pattern in the development of theories and definitions of irony. Pragmatic theory has played a strong role, and a general tendency has been for scholars to describe cases or examples of irony which some prior or competing theory is (in their minds) unable to account for. A more recent handbook definition of verbal irony offered by Herbert Colston weds these theories into a parsimonious and encompassing definition of verbal irony: "Verbal irony thus bears the characteristic of a linguistic creation by a speaker or writer, that somehow expresses some proposition, stance, attitude, description, etc., concerning objective reality, that is somehow contrary to that reality". (Colston, 2017, p. 236)

This definition is thus specific enough to distinguish verbal irony from other forms of figurative language, but also broad enough to include a range of different types of verbal irony. This raises an additional challenge associated with defining verbal irony – there are a number of different types of verbal irony, such as sarcasm, rhetorical questions, hyperbole, understatement, ironic praise, ironic criticism, and more (Gibbs & Colston, 2012). The thorniest among these is the relationship between sarcasm and verbal irony (Kreuz, 2020). Sarcasm is usually seen as a negative, hurtful form of verbal irony (Colston, 2017), but otherwise seems to bear the same characteristics of verbal irony, causing many researchers and laypersons to conflate the two terms (Kreuz, 2020). It is beyond the scope of this work to make an argument either way on this debate, but it is worthwhile to note that many psycholinguistic studies of verbal irony processing and comprehension have used examples of sarcasm in their stimuli.

2 Enter Psycholinguistics: Early Studies of Verbal Irony Processing

Section 1 defined verbal irony and described some of the early pragmatic theories put forth as a means to explain how hearers and readers understand verbal irony. Each of the definitions provided in Section 1 stipulated that an ironic utterance creates a type of contradiction within the context it is made, and thus a hearer or reader needs to cognitively reconcile that contradiction using other available information in order to understand the ironic meaning. As such, it is generally agreed that understanding ironic meaning is a metarepresentational process, which means that irony is a type of inference made in light of the utterance and combined pragmatic and situational knowledge (Gibbs & Colston, 2012). However, the psycholinguistic mechanisms of this inferential process are less agreed upon, which has led to a large number of psycholinguistic studies investigating this process.

One reason for initial interest in using psycholinguistic methods to test models of verbal irony processing can be attributed to the SPM. Recall that based on Gricean conversational maxims, the SPM stipulated that the literal meaning of an ironic utterance would be interpreted first, before a hearer could obtain the ironic meaning. The SPM has thus been referred to as a two-stage (Attardo, 2000; Gibbs & Colston, 2007) or as a literal-first model (Bezuidenhout & Cutting, 2002) of verbal irony processing. The influence of the SPM on subsequent psycholinguistic research cannot be understated and has contributed to one of the most central research questions associated with psycholinguistic investigations of verbal irony: whether a hearer must process the literal/surface meaning of an utterance as a precondition to understanding the figurative, ironic meaning. To test these questions, many of these early psycholinguistic investigations of verbal irony relied on measuring reading and/ or reaction times to text stimuli. These timings were obtained by asking participants to press a key on a keyboard or response button to indicate when they were done reading stimuli or to provide responses. While in hindsight it may be easy to critique these methods for lacking the fine-grained precision of eye-tracking or neurolinguistic methods (see Section 3), the data obtained from these early studies was crucial in driving the direction of the field and providing empirical evidence for these models. And, as will also be shown in Section 3, the use of reading and reaction times are just one way to test the predictions of these models – the reader should take care not to equate particular methods with particular theories throughout this section and the rest.

2.1 Direct Access

In psycholinguistic terms, the SPM predicts that ironic and other figurative language requires more effortful processing when compared to nonfigurative language because two meanings must be processed and considered (i.e., the literal and figurative meanings). These predictions were questioned by Raymond W. Gibbs Jr., who at the time had already published psycholinguistic studies demonstrating readers were able to extract the intended meaning from indirect requests and idiomatic expressions without needing to first interpret a literal meaning (see Gibbs, 1984, for an overview). One of the core arguments raised by Gibbs against the SPM was that many utterances (both figurative and nonfigurative) do not have a clearly identifiable literal meaning, making it difficult to accept a literal-first processing model. Gibbs further hypothesized that because sarcasm was a largely pragmatic phenomenon, pragmatic information (in addition to semantic meaning) would be used immediately by interlocutors when using sarcasm. There would thus be no need for a hearer or reader to always and fully consider the literal meaning of a sarcastic utterance because the larger conversational context would facilitate the interpretation of ironic meaning.

2.1.1 Empirical Tests of the Direct Access View

These arguments were put forth in an early psycholinguistic study conducted by Gibbs as a means to investigate the online, psycholinguistic processing of verbal irony. The article, titled *On the Psycholinguistics of Sarcasm* (Gibbs, 1986b), sought to contrast the predictions of the SPM against the use-mention/

Table 1 Example stimuli from Gibbs (1986b, p. 5)

Negative story context	Sarcastic ending	Nonsarcastic ending
Harry was building an addition to his house. He was working real hard putting in the foundation. His younger brother was supposed to help. But he never showed up. At the end of a long day, Harry's brother finally appeared. Harry was a bit upset with him. Harry said to his brother...	"You're a big help."	"You're not helping me."

Positive story context	Literal ending	Compliment ending
Greg was having trouble with calculus. He had a big exam coming up and he was in trouble. Fortunately, his roommate tutored him on some of the basics. When they were done, Greg felt he'd learned a lot. "Well," he said to his roommate...	"You're a big help."	"Thanks for your help."

echoic theory of irony, described in Section 1.3. The study consisted of six separate experiments which measured reading times of sentences, reaction times for sentence paraphrase true/false judgments, and memory recall of utterances used sarcastically and nonsarcastically.

In the first experiment, participants read a series of stories depicting situations which were either negative (e.g., a younger brother failing to offer promised help to an older brother) or positive (e.g., a university roommate providing free tutoring). The negative stories ended in either a sarcastic (e.g., "you're a big help") or nonsarcastic utterance (e.g., "you're not helping me"). The positive stories ended in either a literal statement (e.g., "you're a big help") or an acknowledgment (e.g., "thanks for the help"). Crucially, the sentence used to create sarcastic meaning in the negative context was the same sentence used literally in the positive contexts (e.g., "you're a big help"), allowing for a direct comparison of processing times for the same utterance in contexts which did and did not bias a sarcastic interpretation (see Table 1).

Participants read the target stories and also made a true/false judgment to paraphrases of the final sentences, with reading times and true/false reaction times analyzed as the dependent variables. The results indicated participants were equally as fast or faster in reading and making judgments for the sarcastic versions of utterances when compared to their literal versions. Because the SPM would predict that the sarcastic uses would take longer to read than the literal uses, Gibbs took these findings as evidence that readers were able to understand sarcastic meaning without needing to first understand the literal meaning of a statement. Gibbs reasoned that because the negative stories provided a pragmatic context supportive of a sarcastic interpretation, participants had no difficulty understanding the sarcasm immediately: "Given adequate information about the speaker's intentions, understanders can comprehend the meaning of sarcastic utterances more or less *directly* [emphasis added]." (Gibbs, 1986b, p. 6). The results from this study thus provided the genesis for what later came to be called the *direct access* view of verbal irony comprehension, in which readers and hearers need not analyze the entire literal meaning of an ironic utterance because pragmatic knowledge of the situation makes a sarcastic or ironic interpretation directly available.

The next two experiments in Gibbs (1986b) tested predictions of the use-mention theory by comparing reading times and true/false paraphrase judgments for sarcastic utterances following either explicit or implicit echoes (Experiment 2) or following situations that did or did not implicitly echo societal norms (Experiment 3). The results indicated that reading and reaction times were quicker for sarcastic utterances following explicit (vs. implicit) echoes as well as for normative (vs. nonnormative) societal values. Aside from providing some empirical support for the use-mention theory of verbal irony, these results unpacked the manner in which pragmatic knowledge was integrated into the processing of verbal irony in that stronger pragmatic cues facilitated sarcasm processing.

As a means to further test how directly pragmatic knowledge was accessed during the processing of sarcasm, Gibbs (1986b) included three more experiments probing participants' memory for sarcastic utterances, with the hypothesis that the pragmatic effect of sarcastic utterances should enhance their memorability. Using the same stimuli from Experiments 1–3, Gibbs asked participants to read the stories and then tested their memory for the utterances used in each story. The results were similar to the first three experiments. Participants remembered sarcastic utterances with greater accuracy and confidence when compared to all other utterances (Experiment 4), and memory recall was more accurate for sarcastic utterances made in reference to an explicit (vs. implicit) echo (Experiment 5) or in reference to a normative (vs. nonnormative) value (Experiment 6).

Gibbs published another 1986 study in which he tested the online processing of indirect sarcastic requests (Gibbs, 1986a). The stimuli included short stories, two-thirds of which depicted situations in which a speaker made an indirect request (e.g., a person wanting their roommate to close a window because it was cold). Half of these stories used a sarcastic indirect request (e.g., "sure is nice and warm in here"), while the other half used a nonsarcastic indirect request (e.g., "why don't you close the window?"). The remaining stories did not include a scenario where a speaker made a request, but still used the same target utterances which were used as sarcastic indirect requests, allowing for a direct comparison of the same utterance used both sarcastically and nonsarcastically. In Experiment 1, participants read a mixture of the stories, sentence by sentence, and then answered whether a paraphrase provided for each story was true or false. Results indicated participants read utterances and made paraphrase decisions significantly faster for the sarcastic indirect requests when compared to both other contexts, providing further support that readers were able to immediately extract the sarcastic meaning without needing to fully consider the literal meaning.

Using the same logic for testing memory recall of sarcastic utterances, Gibbs (1986a) conducted a second experiment to test the memory recall of the three utterance types (sarcastic indirect request, nonsarcastic indirect request, or literal use of the sarcastic indirect request). In Experiment 2, a separate group of participants listened to audio-recorded versions of the stories, and 15 minutes later these participants answered a multiple-choice exam testing the recall of the final utterances used. Participants were asked to choose from among four options (three distractors and the target utterance) and also provide a confidence rating for their choice. Results indicated that participants were more accurate at remembering the sarcastic indirect requests when compared to the nonsarcastic indirect requests, but no significant difference was found for the recall rate between sarcastic and literal uses. However, the confidence ratings were significantly higher for the sarcastic indirect requests when compared to both the nonsarcastic indirect requests and the literal uses. Gibbs interpreted these findings to support the hypothesis that sarcasm would be more meaningful due to its unique pragmatic purpose. Because the audio recordings in Experiment 2 used intonation thought to be associated with sarcasm use (see Section 4.1), a third experiment was conducted in which participants read the stories, rather than hearing them, but the methods were otherwise identical. The results from Experiment 3 matched with those from Experiment 2, suggesting that the memorability of the sarcastic utterances was related to the pragmatic information and not the tone of voice or other manner of presentation.

In sum, the two 1986 studies from Gibbs presented empirical evidence against the predictions of the SPM and have become a cornerstone set of experiments for what is now typically referred to as the direct access view (Colston, 2017; Gibbs & Colston, 2012). Together, the studies provided two key findings: (1) participants were able to immediately and directly access sarcastic meaning when the conversational context supported such meaning (based on reading times), and (2) manipulations to the pragmatic context affected reading times and memory recall, in turn suggesting that pragmatic information was being used during the initial processing of sarcastic utterances. Any differences in processing between sarcastic or nonsarcastic utterances would thus be a function of the pragmatic knowledge available to a listener and *not* the need to first interpret the complete literal meaning of a sarcastic utterance.

2.2 Graded Salience Hypothesis

While Gibbs (1986a, 1986b) provided empirical evidence against the predictions of the SPM, an alternative model to both the SPM and the direct access view was put forth by Rachel Giora. This model, dubbed *the graded salience hypothesis* (GSH), agreed with the direct access model in that ironic (and other figurative) meaning could be directly accessed in certain situations. However, the GSH disagreed as to the reasons why figurative meaning was accessed directly. Giora argued that the most salient meanings of any utterance, figurative or not, will be automatically processed by a listener, and that this process occurs regardless of the pragmatic information available (Giora, 1997).

In this model, salience is an umbrella term which incorporates lexical features such as word frequency, meaning familiarity, conventionality of use, and prototypes (Giora, 2003). The strength of these features individually differs for any one word or utterance, meaning that salience is *graded* along the lexical features of frequency, familiarity, and so on. At a certain threshold, the most salient meanings for both single words and conventionalized sequences of words will be "stored or coded in the mental lexicon" (Giora, 2003, p. 15), resulting in effortless and automatic extraction of meaning associated with that entry. The strength of these features also differs among speakers, suggesting that each language user has their own set of mental encodings.

Crucially, Giora initially argued that for ironic language, the literal meaning was salient and encoded, whereas the ironic meaning was not. As such, processing of ironic language would always be slower because the literal meaning would be automatically activated due to salience. As will be discussed in Section 2.4.1, this view was subsequently relaxed to allow for the possibility of familiar ironies being encoded in the lexicon (as well as other moderating effects). As such, the GSH predicts that regardless of whether the stored meaning is ironic, literal, or something else, that meaning will be automatically activated even in the presence of contextual factors which do not bias such an interpretation.

2.2.1 GSH and Indirect Negation

Giora (2003) described two discrete stages of language processing and how they relate to understanding figurative meaning. In the first stage, top-down contextual and pragmatic information is analyzed in parallel with the bottom-up, automatic activation of encoded lexical meanings (Giora, 2003). During this stage, the salient, encoded meanings of words and utterances are automatically activated while a listener also attends to contextual and pragmatic information. If the automatically activated meaning extracted from the lexicon matches with the pragmatic context, there is no need for additional processing of the utterance. If there is a mismatch, the utterance must be reanalyzed in order to extract alternative potential meanings which exist in the mental lexicon but have not achieved the hard-coded status Giora claimed the most familiar meanings will attain.

The second processing stage is the contextual integration phase, where the initially activated meanings are retained or suppressed in light of the pragmatic context (Giora, 2003). Giora argued that whether a meaning is retained or suppressed is beyond the predictions of the GSH, which only makes predictions regarding the nature of automatic lexical activation. However, when considering the nature of most spoken ironies, Giora put forth an additional hypothesis, known as the *indirect negation* view of verbal irony. The indirect negation view argued that verbal irony is a method for negating meaning without the use of explicit negation markers (Giora, 1995, 2003; Giora et al., 1998, 2013). This is evidenced by the many instances of verbal irony in which the surface level (or literal) meaning of an ironic utterance is made in the positive, such as the fictional example of the friend in a movie theater ("I sure love it when people turn off their cell phones during a movie!"). The indirect negation view argues that this positive meaning is the salient, automatically activated meaning of the utterance, and that a hearer must compare this meaning to the negated version in order to understand the ironic meaning. As such, a cognitive comparison between the positive and negated meanings of utterances, in tandem with recognition of the context, is how many ironic utterances achieve their effects. This explanation may sound similar to the predictions of the SPM but recall that the GSH does not assume the encoded meaning must always be the literal meaning, it is just the case the many ironic utterances invite this comparison as a means to create an ironic effect.

2.2.2 Empirical Tests of the Graded Salience Hypothesis

The predictions of the GSH have been put to test in a number of psycholinguistic studies conducted by Giora and colleagues as well as other researchers (e.g., see Section 3). The earliest of such studies sought to verify the predictions that salient meanings of irony would be initially activated (predicted by the GSH), and that the salient meanings of ironic utterances would be the literal meanings which would be retained during irony processing (predicted by the indirect negation view). In an article titled *Irony: Graded Salience and Indirect Negation*, Giora, et al. (1998) applied the predictions of the GSH and indirect negation view in three reading time experiments. Similar in manner to the 1986 studies by Gibbs, Giora, et al. (1998) placed phrases that could be interpreted either literally or ironically (e.g., *"You are just in time"*) at the end of short paragraphs biasing either an ironic or nonironic reading of the target phrase. In Experiment 1, participants read the phrases line by line and then answered a yes/ no comprehension question about the target phrase. The critical measurement for this experiment was the time difference between initial onset of the ironic or nonironic utterance and when participants pushed a button to move on to the comprehension question. Unlike the results from Gibbs (1986a, 1986b), the results from Giora et al. (1998) Experiment 1 indicated that participants took significantly longer to read the ironic versions of the statements compared to the literal versions of the statement. This was taken as evidence supporting the hypothesis that the ironic meaning was the nonsalient (and thus nonencoded) meaning associated with the target sentences.

Having obtained evidence suggesting the nonironic meanings of the target utterances were the salient meanings, Giora et al. (1998) proceeded to test whether the literal meanings of the utterances were activated when the utterances appeared in ironic contexts. To do so, Experiments 2 and 3 used the same material as Experiment 1, but also included a lexical decision task (wherein participants are asked to judge if a word is real or not). The target words in the lexical decision task were said to be related to either the literal or ironic meaning of the target utterances and were presented to the participants after they read the target utterances. Giora et al. (1998) predicted that response times to the target words should be quicker when the meanings of the word and utterance were similar, which in turn would provide insight as to which meanings of the utterances were active. In Experiment 2, the target words for the lexical decision task were presented either 150 or 1,000 ms after the target utterance. The logic behind the two different intervals was to determine which meanings of the utterance were initially activated during the first stage of processing (150 ms condition) and which still remained after the second, contextual integration phase of processing (1,000 ms condition).

The results from Experiment 2 indicated the response times for words associated with the literal meaning of the utterance were always responded to significantly quicker than those associated with the ironic meaning. This finding was interpreted to mean that the literal meanings of the utterances were activated regardless of the story context (literal or ironic biasing) *or* the interval between the target utterance and the lexical decision task (150 ms or 1,000 ms). These results were taken as further support for the GSH because they suggested the nonironic meaning of an utterance was always activated, and moreover that this meaning was a necessary component of understanding irony. Experiment 3 was identical to Experiment 2 but instead used an interval of 2,000 ms between the target utterance and lexical decision task. The results indicated no significant differences between ironic or literal target words after 2,000 ms in the ironic stories contexts. This was interpreted to mean that after a period of 2,000 ms, the less-salient (i.e., ironic) meanings were now just as active as the salient (i.e., literal meanings), supporting the predictions of the GSH. These results also suggested that during the processing of ironic meaning, the literal meanings were not suppressed but instead held in active memory in order to understand the irony, supporting the predictions of the indirect negation view of irony.

2.3 Clarifying the Direct Access View's Predictions

After these initial studies testing direct access or the GSH, proponents of the direct access view and GSH continued to engage in healthy academic debate and subsequent empirical study (e.g., Gibbs, 2002; Giora, 2002). While Giora and colleagues have continued to publish a series of empirical studies expanding and refining the scope of the GSH (see Section 2.4), Gibbs has published mostly theoretical pieces clarifying his original arguments regarding literal meaning, the SPM, and figurative language processing.

One challenge faced by proponents of the direct access view was that some early criticisms of the model were based on a mischaracterization that the direct access view does not allow for any role of literal meaning during processing, a view Gibbs has continuously strived to correct (Gibbs, 2002, 2005; Gibbs & Colston, 2012). The major points of the direct access view have been that (1) literal meaning itself is in many cases difficult to clearly identify and that (2) in the case of such so-called literal meanings, there is no need to always process the *entire* literal meaning before then being able to arrive at the figurative meaning (Gibbs, 1984, 1994). The main contention is that strength of contextual and pragmatic information will modulate the access to ironic meaning. However, as will be shown in Section 5 and elsewhere, operationalizing the strength of context can be challenging.

Alongside these specific claims about the direct access view is a related argument put forth by Gibbs wherein the privileging of literal meaning as the default, standard mode for language processing and comprehension has led some researchers down the wrong path (Gibbs, 2002). Because researchers had categorized different meanings into qualitatively different types, such as literal, ironic, or metaphorical, there was a tendency to thus assume that these types of meanings would require different processing mechanisms, with differences in processing *times* somehow reflecting these different mechanisms. As is compellingly argued in several publications, the idea that the brain switches among qualitatively different language processing architectures for literal, figurative, and other types of meaning may not be realistic. While it may indeed be the case that ironic or figurative language use does sometimes take longer than a literal approximation, this increased processing difficulty may reflect extended variations of the same fundamental process. In other words, figurative, literal, and all other instances of language use are still processed in the same manner – through a combined consideration of both semantic and pragmatic information available to the listener (Gibbs, 1994, 2002; Gibbs & Colston, 2012).

2.4 Expanding the Graded Salience Hypothesis

Early conceptualizations of the GSH assumed that ironic meaning was nonsalient and thus not encoded in the mental lexicon. This assumption was adjusted in light of further theoretical consideration as well as new empirical evidence, which suggested some instances of language may indeed be interpreted as ironic by default (Giora, 2021; Giora et al., 2013; Giora, Drucker, et al., 2015).

2.4.1 Salient and Familiar Ironic Meaning

Giora and Fein (1999) acknowledged that familiar ironies may actually be coded in the mental lexicon, resulting in automatic activation of ironic meaning. They further argued that familiar ironies could have more than a single encoded meaning, suggesting that both the literal and the ironic meaning would be activated in parallel during initial processing. To test these ideas, Giora and Fein (1999) included ironic utterances categorized into familiar and unfamiliar ironies based on a familiarity pretest. The pretest involved undergraduate students summarizing the meanings of decontextualized sentences, and any sentence identified as ironic by over half of the students was classified as a familiar irony. As an example, the phrase "very funny" was rated as a familiar use of irony compared to "I think you should eat something."

The familiar and less familiar ironies were presented in contexts biasing either an ironic or literal reading of the target utterances. Experiment 1 used methods similar to those used in Giora et al. (1998), wherein participants read target stories and then completed a lexical decision task, with target words said

Table 2 Example stimuli from Giora and Fein (1999, p. 245), with target utterances bolded

Bias	Familiar ironies	Ironic target	Literal target
Ironic	Iris was walking on her own in the dark alley, when all of a sudden a hand was laid on her back. Startled, she turned around to find out that the hand was her young brother who sneaked behind her to frighten her. She said to him: "**Very funny.**"		
		annoying	*amusing*
Literal	Tal and Ortal, the twins, wanted to go to the movies. Their mother recommended a movie she had seen shortly before. When they came home, she was eager to know how they found the movie. They both agreed: "**Very funny.**"		

Bias	Less familiar ironies	Ironic target	Literal target
Ironic	After he had finished eating pizza, falafel, ice cream, wafers, and half of the cream cake his mother had baked for his brother Benjamin's birthday party, Moshe started eating coated peanuts. His mother said to him: "**Moshe, I think you should eat something.**"		
		stop	*little*
Literal	At two o'clock in the afternoon, Moshe started doing his homework and getting prepared for his Bible test. When his mother came home from work at eight p.m., Moshe was still seated at his desk, looking pale. His mother said to him: "**Moshe, I think you should eat something.**"		

to be associated with either the ironic or literal meanings of the utterances (see Table 2). The interval between the target utterance and the lexical decision task was set to either 150 or 1,000 ms. The results for less familiar ironies indicated that in the 150 ms interval condition, target words associated with literal meaning were responded to significantly faster in both the ironic and literal biasing contexts. In the 1,000 ms condition, there was no significant difference between literal and ironic target words in the ironic contexts, while literal targets were responded to quicker in the literal contexts. In contrast, they reported no significant differences in response times for target words when comparing the *familiar* ironies to their literal counterparts. These results were taken as supportive of the GSH because the literal, salient meanings of the less familiar ironies were active during initial processing (150 ms), whereas facilitation for the less-salient ironic meaning appeared only after a 1,000 ms delay. A second experiment confirmed the results obtained from Experiment 1 were not due to differences between the story contexts used for the familiar and less familiar ironies.

The Giora and Fein (1999) study thus revised the initial predictions of the GSH to allow for the possibility that some ironic uses may indeed have a coded figurative or ironic interpretation in the mental lexicon. Their study also introduced a procedure for identifying familiar ironies based on rating studies performed on the stimuli before the psycholinguistic tests. Note that ironies were categorized in a binary nature, as either familiar or unfamiliar. There may be further differences among the two categories which further expand the degree of familiarity along a continuum, rather than as a binary choice.

2.4.2 Expecting Irony

Because the GSH predicted contextual factors would never block the automatic activation of salient meaning, further studies from Giora and colleagues probed the strength of contextual influence on the processing of ironic meaning. One potentially strong contextual influence would be if a hearer encounters multiple ironic statements from the same source during communication. The repeated exposure to verbal irony may in turn create an expectation for irony from the speaker, providing a strong contextual pressure in favor of an ironic interpretation. Conversely, if readers or listeners still automatically activate the salient (i.e., nonironic or literal) meaning of an utterance while anticipating irony, this would be further evidence suggesting that the salient meanings were automatically activated, regardless of contextual influence.

This question was put to the test in Giora et al. (2007). Based on the GSH, Giora et al. (2007) predicted that because unfamiliar ironic meaning is not encoded in the mental lexicon, encountering a prior ironic context would still not allow for the direct processing of ironic meaning when encountering a subsequent unfamiliar ironic utterance. To test this prediction, Giora et al. (2007) created fictional dialogues between two speakers biasing a penultimate utterance to be ironic or nonironic. They further manipulated the dialogues so that in half of the dialogues one of the speakers made an ironic remark approximately halfway through the conversation. Reading time results from Experiment 1 indicated that target utterances were read significantly slower when placed in the ironic versus literal conditions, regardless of whether or not the ironic condition contained a prior ironic statement. These results thus suggested that anticipating irony still did not prevent the automatic activation of the salient, nonironic meaning.

Experiments 2–4 used a new set of stories in which the final (rather than the penultimate) sentence of each story was biased to be ironic or literal. The target sentences each included a lexical item thought to carry the brunt of the ironic or literal meaning (e.g., the word *terrific* in the sentence "this is *terrific* news!"). The final sentences were presented one word at a time in order to gather reading times for the target words as well as subsequent words. Giora et al. (2007) also included a lexical decision task where participants made judgments to target words said to be related to the literal or ironic meaning of the utterance (the short/long intervals in this study were 250 ms and 1,400 ms). As a response to criticism that lexical decision results from prior studies were unfairly biased toward lexical relationships in the literal contexts and inferential relationships in ironic contexts (Gibbs, 2002), Giora et al. (2007) chose word targets which did not contain lexical associations to the target words in the utterances, and instead reflected conceptual similarity to the literal or ironic meanings (as well as a third, unrelated word condition).

Results from Experiment 2 indicated that reading times for the critical words in the target utterances were similar in both the ironic and literal contexts, but reading times for words appearing *after* the critical words were slower in the ironic contexts. This spillover effect was interpreted to support the claim that initial lexical access was the literal meaning, and that subsequent processing was required to understand the ironic meaning in the ironic contexts. Moreover, there was no significant facilitation of the literal or ironic word targets (vs. unrelated) in the 250 ms interval condition, whereas the literal-related targets were facilitated in both the ironic and literal contexts after the 1,400 ms interval. These results were taken as evidence that (1) the word targets did not reflect lexical associations (because there was no facilitation during early processing) and (2) the literal meaning was activated in both instances, as predicted by the GSH. Experiments 3 and 4 then used the same material as Experiment 2, but also manipulated the stimuli so that half of the stories created an expectation for irony, similar in manner to Experiment 1. The interval between the target sentence and the lexical decision task was changed to 750 ms (Experiment 3) or 1,000 ms (Experiment 4). Results found that reaction times for literal target words were always quicker, regardless of story context (ironic vs. literal), and regardless of whether the ironic stories primed an expectation for irony.

Fein et al. (2015) replicated these findings using the same stimuli as Giora et al. (2007), but modified to include more explicit markers of irony (through the use of adverbs such as "derisively" associated with the ironic speaker). The Giora et al. (2007) and Fein et al. (2015) studies thus provided evidence that at least one contextual variable, the expectation of irony, did not appear to influence subsequent processing of irony, even within the same conversation. Instead, the salient, coded meaning was always activated, supporting the predictions of the GSH.

The Fein et al. (2015) study also included yet another refinement to the GSH which argued for three different possible encodings of meaning in the lexicon, rather than a binary between encoded/not encoded. Specifically, salient meanings are meanings coded in the mental lexicon and "enjoy prominence" (p. 3) due to conventionality, frequency, or other usage-based influences. Less-salient meanings are those coded in the mental lexicon but are less frequent or conventional. Nonsalient meanings are novel meanings *not* encoded in the lexicon at all, and must be constructed in real time, resulting in either a "salience-based or a nonsalient *interpretation*" (p. 3, emphasis original). As always, salience makes no distinction between literal and figurative meaning.

2.4.3 Default Nonliteral Interpretations

Another key contribution from the research conducted by Giora and colleagues came to be known as the *defaultness hypothesis* (Giora et al., 2013; Giora, Givoni, et al., 2015). This hypothesis emerged from the observation that, under certain conditions, some negated utterances produce metaphorical, sarcastic, and other nonliteral interpretations by default (Giora et al., 2013). According to this view, the negation of overly positive attributes in sentences such as "intelligent he is not" attenuates the positive attributes in a manner which prompts a consideration (rather than suppression) of the negative elements, resulting in a sarcastic interpretation (Giora, 2021; Giora et al., 2018).

How can the defaultness hypothesis coexist with the predictions of the GSH, which holds that unfamiliar sarcastic or ironic meanings are nonsalient and thus not encoded in the mental lexicon? The answer is that the defaultness hypothesis raised a crucial distinction between default *meanings* and default *interpretations*. The GSH predicts that salient and familiar *meanings* are encoded in the mental lexicon and accessed directly regardless of contextual information. However, the GSH also recognizes not all utterances are associated with encoded meanings, and when this is the case, a listener constructs an *interpretation* of the utterance by drawing on nonencoded information in the lexicon (Giora, 2003). As such, the utterances which negate highly positive attributes are *interpreted* as sarcastic by default.

To be interpreted as sarcastic by default, utterances must first have the potential to be ambiguous in that the utterance could be interpreted either ironically or literally, depending upon the context in which it is made. These utterances must then adhere to three additional constraints. First, the utterance must be novel in that it is not part of a conventionalized formulaic sequence which would be associated with an encoded meaning in the lexicon. Second, the phrase must lack obvious semantic or syntactic incongruity. Third, the utterance must be devoid of any paralinguistic, gestural, or other contextual cues which may mark a sarcastic intention (Giora, 2021; Giora et al., 2013, 2018). The defaultness hypothesis then makes two predictions for utterances which meet the aforementioned criteria. First, these utterances will be identified as sarcastic (via survey ratings) when presented in isolation. Second, the default sarcastic interpretation will be automatically interpreted regardless of context, so that these utterances will thus be processed quicker when presented in contexts which support a sarcastic versus a literal interpretation (Giora et al., 2013).

Giora and colleagues conducted a number of studies testing these predictions. The general procedure in these studies was to first locate examples of utterances which meet the set of criteria listed in the previous paragraph, sometimes using large corpora (e.g., Giora et al., 2014). These utterances were provided to research participants without any context, who then rated the utterances for degrees of sarcasm using rating scales which spanned from *highly sarcastic* to *not sarcastic at all*. After identifying the utterances interpreted as sarcastic in this decontextualized setting, the utterances were then used as stimuli in reading time experiments (Giora et al., 2013; Giora, Drucker, et al., 2015; Giora, Givoni, et al., 2015). In these experiments, utterances were presented in story contexts which biased either a sarcastic or literal interpretation. Findings showed that, following the predictions of the defaultness hypothesis, utterances rated as highly sarcastic when presented in isolation were also read significantly quicker when presented in a context supporting a sarcastic (vs. literal) interpretation. As such, these studies provided evidence indicating phrases such as "clever she is not" (Giora et al., 2013, p. 90), "he is not the most organized student" (Giora, Givoni, et al., 2015, p. 291), and "intelligence is not his forte" (Giora, Drucker, et al., 2015, p. 174) were all interpreted as sarcastic by default. The logic behind the defaultness hypothesis and a more detailed overview of these studies (as well as studies testing metaphor) can be found in Giora (2021).

2.4.4 Evaluating the GSH

The GSH has withstood a number of empirical investigations conducted by both Giora and colleagues as well as subsequent researchers employing more fine-grained methods such as eye tracking (see Section 3). Despite these subsequent tests, core questions regarding the predictions of the GSH persist. As a linguist, Giora drew from a range of other linguistic research such as investigations of lexical ambiguity resolution and theories of construction grammar in order to make her arguments (Giora, 2003). Nonetheless, there still exists some difficulty in being able to clearly operationalize the concept of salience and identify whether a meaning is encoded in one's lexicon or not (Filik et al., 2014). Moreover, while the incorporation of the distinction between coded *meanings* and *interpretations* provided by the defaultness hypothesis seems to address contradictory results showing automatic activation of nonsalient ironic meanings, it does little to resolve the question of how to determine if a meaning is coded or not. The claim that ironic meaning is nonsalient and thus not coded in the lexicon is nonetheless both theoretically and empirically interesting and is likely to continue propelling research in this area.

2.5 Parallel-Constraint Satisfaction

Although the direct access view and GSH comprised a good portion of the early reading time studies of verbal irony, there were also a number of additional researchers joining the conversation and using psycholinguistic methods to test the processing of verbal irony (e.g., Schwoebel et al., 2000). Some of these researchers voiced a dissatisfaction for the way in which many psycholinguistic studies of verbal irony did not account for a number of social and pragmatic variables which are available during naturalistic uses of verbal irony (Katz, 2005, 2017). As an alternative to the direct access view and GSH, the parallel-constraint satisfaction approach was proposed (Katz, 2005; Pexman, 2005, 2008). Like direct access and graded salience, the constraint-satisfaction approach also rejects the idea that literal meaning must always be computed to arrive at an ironic interpretation, instead suggesting listeners simultaneously (i.e., in *parallel*) take stock of a variety of cues from the context, the utterance, and the speaker (i.e., the *constraints*). The range of cues is relatively large, encompassing linguistic information from the statement (such as familiarity), social information from the speaker (such as their attitudes), knowledge of prior events, and more (Pexman, 2008). The constraint-satisfaction approach argues that all of these cues are processed in real time, representing a probabilistic network of coactivated information similar in nature to other connectionist models of language processing. As such, linguistic input activates different cues, which work in tandem to construct the best interpretation based on the whole of information available, arriving at an ironic (or other) interpretation as soon as specific constraints have been met (Pexman, 2008).

Unlike the direct access view and GSH, the constraint-satisfaction approach does not make clear predictions regarding whether verbal irony will be processed any slower or any faster than nonironic uses. Instead, processing times will vary as a function of the cues available to the reader (Pexman, 2008). As such, early empirical research in this area set about testing how different contextual and pragmatic cues affected processing times for verbal irony. In particular, social information was a core consideration of the proponents of the constraint-satisfaction model.

2.5.1 Empirical Tests of the Constraint-Satisfaction Approach

Although there is no mention made specifically to the constraint-satisfaction approach within, a reading time study by Pexman et al. (2000) is commonly cited as the first psycholinguistic study providing empirical evidence in favor of the constraint-satisfaction approach. The Pexman et al. (2000) study was based on a prior offline norming study which found evidence that social stereotypes inherent to different occupations influenced whether participants interpreted statements such as "children are precious gems" to be metaphorical or ironic (Katz & Pexman, 1997). Specifically, fictional characters from certain occupations were identified as stereotypically more likely to be sarcastic (e.g., comedians, truck drivers), whereas others were more likely to use metaphor (e.g., artists, nurses). Using a series of statements in the form of *A is/ verbs a B* (e.g., *her home is an oasis*), Katz & Pexman (1997) found that attributing statements to fictional speakers of differing occupations biased interpretations of utterances toward ironic or metaphorical readings, and these biases matched the perceptions obtained via ratings of those different occupations.

The Pexman et al. (2000) study then tested whether the information about a speaker's occupation would influence the online processing of verbal irony (and metaphor). Based on the material used in Katz and Pexman (1997), target statements were placed in contexts which biased the statement to be ironic (counterfactual with context), metaphorical (congruent with context), or neutral (neither counterfactual nor congruent). The fictional speakers were identified in the story contexts to be either from a high-irony occupation, a high-metaphor occupation, or no occupational information was provided. Additionally, half of the target statements were identified as familiar metaphors based on a prior rating test (Table 3).

Table 3 Sample stimuli from Pexman et al. (2000, p. 208), with target utterances
bolded

Text stimuli	Condition
A truck driver and a friend, Robin, were talking about a comment that Robin had made to her boss that day. Robin's comment had been scornfully rejected by her boss. The truck driver said: **"That comment hit the bull's eye."** Robin nodded in response to her friend's comment.	- High-irony occupation - Irony inviting context - Familiar target statement
While Andrew and a nurse were having coffee at an outdoor cafe, a man was panhandling in the street nearby. The panhandler smiled at everyone he asked for money. He seemed to be getting a lot of money from the people he asked. The nurse commented that: **"His smiles are canopeners."** Andrew sipped his coffee.	- High-metaphor occupation - Metaphor inviting context - Unfamiliar target statement
Casey and a friend had both received Christmas cards from an acquaintance. Referring to the acquaintance, Casey's friend said: **"His Christmas cards are progress charts."** Casey and his friend then talked about their Christmas plans.	- No occupational information - Neutral context - Unfamiliar target statement

Participants read the stories one word at a time while their reading times for
each individual word were recorded. Key measures included average reading
times for words in the first half of the target utterances (i.e., the A in the A is/
verbs a B structure), reading times for words in the second half of the target
utterances (i.e., the B in the A is/*verbs a B* structure), and two measures of
spillover times after the target utterances. Results included two key effects.
First, reading times for the last word of the target utterance were significantly
longer when the speaker was from a high-irony occupation (vs. no occupational
information), which was taken as evidence that speaker information was integrated during immediate processing of the utterance. The longer reading times
for high-irony occupations suggested the utterances were initially interpreted as
metaphors but changed to irony in light of social information about the
speaker's occupation. Second, an additional three-way interaction indicated
that for contexts involving high-metaphor speakers, word reading times were
stable in both metaphorical and irony inviting contexts for all four of the target
regions. Conversely, for those stories including high-irony speakers, spillover
effects were found in that reading times were longer for the words after the

target utterance, suggesting participants were still integrating social information about the speaker after reading the target phrase. As such, the Pexman et al. (2000) study provided some evidence that speaker occupation was taken into consideration during immediate processing of target utterances as well as afterward.

It is worth briefly clarifying how this study might lend support to the constraint-satisfaction view. Essentially, three potential constraints on figurative language processing were tested: speaker occupation, contextual bias, and utterance familiarity. All three of these constraints exerted influence on the processing of the target utterances, and also to different degrees, such as whether the effects were related to reading times immediately or afterward (see Katz, 2005 for a thorough discussion of this study and its relevance for the parallel-constraint view).

3 Broadening the Scope: Later Psycholinguistic Studies

The early psycholinguistic research investigating verbal irony mainly used reading times for sentences or words as a measure of online processing. These measures were used in combination with comprehension measures such as true/false judgments for paraphrased meanings or lexical decision tasks using words thought to be associated with ironic or nonironic uses. Along with the methodological advances in psycholinguistics it was thus inevitable that later researchers would seek to apply more fine-grained measures of language processing to the study of verbal irony. For instance, the ability for eye-tracking methods to measure rereading of specific words and regions in a text was applied to the question of whether ironic uses of target utterances first required processing the literal meaning. Accordingly, there now exist a large number of studies that have employed eye tracking as a means to investigate various aspects of verbal irony processing (Olkoniemi & Kaakinen, 2021). While the primary goal of some of these studies have been to compare the predictions of the SPM, direct access, and GSH (Filik et al., 2014; Filik & Moxey, 2010), others have simultaneously tested the role of additional influences on verbal irony processing, such as cognitive individual differences (Kaakinen et al., 2014; Olkoniemi et al., 2016). Neurolinguistic methods such as event-related potentials (ERP) and functional magnetic resonance imaging (fMRI) were also applied for similar reasons (Regel et al., 2011; Spotorno et al., 2012).

The desire to apply new methods to investigate verbal irony processing brought with it an influx of additional researchers, almost all of whom were not associated with the original formulations of the early psycholinguistic models described in Section 2. Divorced from any ownership over these models, these subsequent researchers also began asking new research questions as well as exploring factors beyond a dual or single-stage model of processing, which had become relatively standard operating procedure. In this manner, the research described in this section (as well as later sections) reflects a maturation of the psycholinguistic study of verbal irony. Crucially, this maturation is a constellation of these influences: new methods, new researchers, and new questions. As such, any subsequent organization of studies around methods is a matter of convenience and should not be taken as a signal that only certain methods lends themselves to certain models and/or questions.

3.1 Using Eye Tracking to Compare DA, GSH, and SPM

Ruth Filik and colleagues were among the first to employ eye tracking as a method to study verbal irony processing. A series of experiments run from their lab have empirically tested many of the theoretical predictions regarding verbal irony processing. Their experiments represent both methodological improvements through the use of eye tracking but also in terms of stimuli design and careful operationalization of the predictions put forth by the different theories.

3.1.1 The First Eye-Tracking Study of Verbal Irony Processing

The first study to track eye movements during verbal irony processing was Filik and Moxey (2010). Their overall goal was to test predictions made by the SPM, the direct access view, and the GSH by measuring the eye movements of participants while they read utterances biased toward literal or ironic meanings. While this approach was similar to the studies reviewed in Section 2 in that they compared the same utterances placed in literal or ironic biasing contexts, Filik and Moxey (2010) also manipulated the target utterances so that the utterances contained either positive quantifiers (e.g., many people) or negative quantifiers (e.g., not many people). Positive quantifiers include the set of referents for which the statement is true (e.g., many people finished = the people who finished), whereas negative quantifiers are the opposite (e.g., not many people finished = the people who did not finish).

Filik and Moxey (2010) hypothesized that ironic use of these positive and negative quantifiers would reverse their polarity and thus also change the salient referents. For instance, if someone ironically stated "clearly many people came to the show" in light of an empty auditorium, the ironic interpretation would be that the speaker was referring to the lack of attendees (i.e., the people who did *not* come to the show, a meaning associated with a *negative* use of the quantifier). Based on this hypothesis, Filik and Moxey

(2010) created stories including positive or negative quantifiers biased to be ironic or nonironic, depending upon the story context. They also included pronominal statements after the target utterances which either did or did not align with the quantifier in the target utterance. For example, one of the target utterances was "I see many people have come to your party," which was spoken in an ironic context (an empty party) or a literal context (a full party). The responses to the target utterance either referred to the positive referent ("they heard about the free drinks") or the negative referent ("they couldn't get babysitters"). A corresponding version of the story using the negative quantifier ("I see not many people have come to your party") was also shown with the same two responses (see Table 4).

In this design, the online processing of both the target utterances and the responses to the utterances were of interest. The authors described that for the target utterances, the direct access view would predict that the ironic utterances would require no more effort to process than their literal uses, while both the SPM and the GSH would predict greater processing difficulty for the ironic uses (albeit for different reasons). While this data would reveal a more fine-grained picture into how the same utterances were processed both literally and ironically, the processing of the subsequent responses to the target utterances would reveal which meanings were active *after* reading the target utterances. This data would allow the researchers to further distinguish among the predictions of the SPM and GSH. Filik and Moxey (2010) claimed that because the SPM argued for the suppression of literal meaning and the direct access view held that there is no need to access the literal meaning, processing behavior for responses made to ironic utterances after positive or negative quantifiers would be the converse of the literal stories (because only the ironic meaning would be active). As for the GSH, there would be no difference in processing behavior between the literal and ironic uses of the utterances, because the literal (salient) meaning should always be activated.

Three different eye-tracking measures were used: first pass reading times (to capture initial processing), regression path times (to capture rereadings), and total reading times (to capture global processing time). These measures were calculated for three regions of the target utterances (biased to be ironic or literal). Results indicated no significant differences for both first pass and regression path times for all three measured regions. Total reading times, however, were significantly higher for ironic uses in all three regions of the target utterances, which the authors took as evidence that participants tended to reread utterances when used ironically.

The responses to the target utterances were also split into three regions, but only data for the portion of the utterance which disambiguated the pronominal

Table 4 Sample stimulus from Filik and Moxey (2010, p. 423) Bolded words
represent manipulations to bias ironic or nonironic reading. Words in brackets
show options for [positive/negative] quantifier referents

Condition	Text stimuli
Nonironic, positive quantifier (many)	It was raining; Sarah looked round the stadium at the **packed stalls**. "I see many people have come to support their team," she exclaimed. "They [probably wish they watched it on TV instead / are probably watching it on TV instead]," replied the manager. The match was about to start.
Ironic, positive quantifier (many)	It was raining; Sarah looked round the stadium at the **relatively empty stalls**. "I see many people have come to support their team," she exclaimed. "They [probably wish they watched it on TV instead / are probably watching it on TV instead]," replied the manager. The match was about to start.
Nonironic, negative quantifier (not many)	It was raining; Sarah looked round the stadium at the **relatively empty stalls**. "I see not many people have come to support their team," she exclaimed. "They [probably wish they watched it on TV instead / are probably watching it on TV instead]," replied the manager. The match was about to start.
Ironic not, negative quantifier (many)	It was raining; Sarah looked round the stadium at the **packed stalls**. "I see not many people have come to support their team," she exclaimed. "They [probably wish they watched it on TV instead / are probably watching it on TV instead]," replied the manager. The match was about to start.

referent (e.g., they heard *about the free drinks*) and the subsequent attribution of
the referent to a speaker (e.g., *replied the friend*) were analyzed. For the
disambiguating portion, again only total reading times showed significant
effects. Responses to the nonironic target utterances which contained referents
congruent with the previous quantifier were read significantly quicker than
those which were incongruent, which was an expected finding for literal uses.
Conversely, no significant differences were found for the ironic responses,

which Filik and Moxey (2010) interpreted as evidence that both the ironic and literal meaning of the utterances were equally available. Finally, the attribution portion of the responses exhibited the greatest amount of processing differences between the ironic and nonironic uses. Essentially, literal utterances which used quantifiers congruent with the pronominal referent in the response required less reading time and fewer regressions than all other conditions. Ironic utterances which used quantifiers *not* congruent with the pronominal referent were faster than all other conditions aside from the literal uses. In other words, in equally congruent quantifier conditions, responses to the ironic utterances required more processing effort.

The use of eye-tracking techniques to measure verbal irony processing while leveraging a separate linguistic phenomena in the Filik and Moxey (2010) study helped to address some of the methodological concerns associated with reading times as measures of processing and lexical decision responses as measures of meaning activation. An additional novel finding was that processing difficulty appeared to be associated with rereading of the ironic utterances, something the raw measures of reading time were not able to capture. In terms of support for the prior psycholinguistic models, Filik and Moxey (2010) argued that their results best aligned with the predictions of the GSH and provided no evidence in favor of the direct access view (note, however, their description of the direct access view in this study may represent a mischaracterization of the predictions of the direct access view, see Section 2.3).

3.1.2 Rereading Irony

Shortly after the Filik and Moxey (2010) study, Kaakinen et al. (2014) published a study including an experiment designed to test the predictions of the SPM, direct access view, GSH, and the constraint-satisfaction views (Experiment 1). They contrasted the predictions of these views based on whether each theory predicted literal meaning must be processed first (SPM, GSH for unfamiliar ironies) and also whether the ironic interpretation should be immediate given a supportive context (direct access, constraint-satisfaction) or delayed (GSH, SPM). To measure these differences, Kaakinen et al. (2014) calculated measures to reflect the scope of eye movements during the initial reading of an utterance as well as any additional rereadings. Their results found significant differences in that ironic uses of target utterances were associated with a significantly higher likelihood of being reread during the initial encounter and were also more likely to be looked back upon from other segments of the text. Kaakinen et al. (2014) emphasized that these results indicated additional processing costs associated with irony, and also that these processing costs appeared early during processing and were associated with the target utterances.

The finding that irony was associated with more rereadings in this study (as well as Filik and Moxey, 2010) provided an additional point of empirical evidence suggesting ironic utterances were being reanalyzed during reading. This rereading behavior has been interpreted as evidence in favor the GSH over the direct access view, not necessarily because it indicates greater processing effort, but also because it demonstrates how an utterance used ironically is more likely to be considered multiple times, suggesting the initial meaning was being reconsidered. Moreover, the results from the Filik and Moxey (2010) and Kaakinen et al. (2014) studies also indicated that greater processing costs for irony are experienced during both early and late stages of processing. Both studies made the point that previous research using moving window or self-paced reading methods which included results congruent with the direct access (i.e., the Gibbs 1986 studies) or constraint-satisfaction accounts (i.e., Pexman et al. 2000) may have been due to the methodological differences involved.

3.1.3 Eye Tracking and Replications of the Graded Salience Hypothesis

Filik and colleagues continued to conduct further studies testing the predictions of the SPM, direct access view, and GSH. In doing so, they revisited some of the expanded components of the GSH, such as the role of familiarity and expect-ations for irony (Filik et al., 2014; Ţurcan & Filik, 2016), as well as returning to the predictions of the echoic theory of irony. In some regards, these studies served as additional verification that the extensions made to the GSH based on reading times and lexical decision tasks (see Sections 2.2 and 2.4) replicated when using eye-tracking methods.

For instance, as a test of familiar ironies, Filik et al. (2014) compared eye movements (Experiment 1) of participants reading familiar and unfamiliar ironies. Stimuli included stories containing target utterances which differed by a single word to bias an ironic or literal interpretation. Results demonstrated that participants spent more time reading the ironic utterances when compared to their literal counterparts, but no differences were found between familiar ironies and their literal matches. As such, this approach worked to further attest that some ironies may be familiar enough to have meanings encoded in the mental lexicon per the predictions of the GSH.

Ţurcan and Filik (2016) further modeled the effects of context via expect-ations for irony by manipulating the degree of expectation in a text. One of the goals of this study was to empirically test a formula derived by Utsumi (2000) designed to model the effects of context on verbal irony processing while also further testing the predictions of the SPM and GSH. In Experiment 1, explicit or implicit expectations were attributed to a speaker in a text, and that expectation was either met or violated by another speaker's actions. Responses to the violated or met expectation were controlled to be ironic or literal, and results from eye-tracking data indicated that the literal uses were always read faster than the ironic uses. Because there was no effect of contextual expectation, this suggested context did not facilitate ironic meaning understanding, which is in line with the predictions of the GSH. A second experiment then modeled familiar versus unfamiliar ironies, with results indicating that familiar ironies were processed as fast as their literal uses (whereas unfamiliar ironies were slower), but this facilitation waned during later stages of processing. In all, this study demonstrated that contextual expectations did not influence irony processing, and that familiar ironies were processed as quickly as their literal uses, providing further support for the predictions of the GSH.

As may come as no surprise, Filik and colleagues also tested the claims of the defaultness hypothesis using eye-tracking methods (Filik et al., 2018). To do so, they constructed a set of stories which contrasted affirmative versus negative versions of utterances to be biased either sarcastically or literally. They again measured eye movements during initial and later stages of reading for different areas of the target utterances. The results broadly supported the predictions of the defaultness hypothesis, in that literal affirmatives were read faster than both literal negatives and sarcastic affirmatives, whereas sarcastic negatives were read faster than negative literals and sarcastic affirmatives. Another key result was that these effects manifested primarily during second-pass readings and only for the latter portions of the utterances, which contrasted with earlier research showing immediate effects of irony recognition (e.g., Filik et al., 2014). One potential reason for the difference was the distinction between default negative sarcasms compared to stimuli used in the prior studies, such as familiar and unfamiliar ironies.

3.1.4 Other Eye-Tracking Studies

In a departure from testing iterative predictions of the GSH, Ṭurcan and Filik (2017) looked back on the predictions made by the use-mention or echoic theory of verbal irony, pointing out that Gibbs (1986b) was likely the only published study to empirically test the effect of echoic mention on verbal irony processing. In a similar fashion to their other studies, they created short stories designed to bias an ironic or literal interpretation. The stories were also manipulated so that half-contained explicit echoic antecedents related to the ironic or literal utterance, and the ironies were also separated into familiar and unfamiliar ironies. In this manner, the study was able to test predictions made by the SPM, the echoic mention theory, and the GSH. Results indicated some support for the echoic mention theory in that target utterances associated with explicit echoes were processed faster, but this held true for both the ironic and the literal versions of the stimuli. Moreover, no key differences were found in processing times for critical regions of unfamiliar ironic and literal target utterances, providing evidence counter to the predictions of the GSH.

In a bit of a shakeup to the usual manner of text presentation in studies of verbal irony, Olkoniemi et al. (2019) questioned whether the typical placement of the target utterance near the end of a story might have an influence on processing. Specifically, they questioned whether processing difficulty typically reported for sarcastic versus literal uses of target utterances was a function of the processing of sarcastic meaning or if it was due to the lack of local paragraph coherence. To answer this question, they created contexts in which a target utterance (e.g., "what a great concert!)" was placed either before (context last) or after (context first) the portions of stories which biased the utterances toward a literal or sarcastic meaning. As such, when the target utterance was placed before the contextual information, the ironic or literal meaning of the target utterance would only be made clear when reading the context which came after reading it, allowing for the authors to separate any effects related to incongruity of local paragraph cohesion. For the context first condition, results matched with prior research in that higher first pass rereading was found for sarcastic versus literal uses of the target utterances. In the context last condition, greater regression path durations were reported for sarcastic versus literal text, but this time for the statements coming *after* the target utterances. Another key difference was that in the context first condition, participants looked back to the target utterance more for sarcastic versus literal uses, but this effect was not found for the equivalent utterances in the context last condition. These findings were interpreted to suggest that the processing of sarcasm in part required a reconsideration of the target utterances, which may support theoretical claims of the SPM.

3.1.5 Key Contributions from Eye Tracking

There are more eye-tracking studies which have not been summarized in this section. Fortunately, a recently published systematic review of eye-tracking studies of verbal irony processing provides some cohesion to the bolus of studies discussed in this section (Olkoniemi & Kaakinen, 2021). Olkoniemi and Kaakinen (2021) focused on ten published eye-tracking studies which were similar enough in methods and stimuli to compare. They analyzed a series of early and late measures of verbal irony processing across the studies. Results of their analysis found no clear pattern of early-stage processing associated with verbal irony. In contrast, they found consistent effects indicating that verbal irony tends to elicit more rereadings and is more difficult to understand than literal equivalents. Their review also provides succinct summaries of how different context-related, text-related, and reader-related questions have been addressed in the eye-tracking literature, much of which has been (or will be) reviewed in this work.

The eye-tracking literature has made important contributions to the understanding of verbal irony processing and provided several methodological advances to the field. The largest contribution from this work is likely providing compelling evidence to suggest that verbal irony, in general, requires more effortful processing when compared to literal uses of the same utterances. The specific finding that verbal irony elicits a greater number of rereadings indicates the surface form of irony may need to be processed more than one time. What also seems clear is that this knowledge of an additional processing cost has not yet settled theoretical debates.

3.2 What's the Difference? Individual Differences and Verbal Irony

Another tack taken by some eye-tracking researchers has been to model a range of cognitive individual differences among readers as they process ironic and literal uses of utterances. As such, these studies demonstrated innovation both in the continued use of eye-tracking measures but also in their attempts to explore cognitive features of participants which may have influenced the results of prior research. The cognitive differences which have been modeled in the published literature include working memory capacity (WMC), need for cognition (NFC), self-reported sarcasm use, and the ability to process and recognize emotions. WMC is a well-studied cognitive individual difference and is defined as the mental capacity to hold information in short-term memory while also completing an additional cognitive task (Cowan, 2005). Individuals with higher working memory are thought to have access to more cognitive resources with which to complete tasks, such as processing and comprehending language. Need for cognition is thought to reflect an individual's tendency to engage in (and enjoy) cognitively difficult tasks, and is measured using a survey which asks participants to rate their level of agreement with certain statements, such as "I only think as hard as I have to" (Cacioppo et al., 1984). The sarcasm self-report scale is an instrument designed to measure an individual's use of sarcastic irony and was validated using principal components analysis (Ivanko et al., 2004). The ability to recognize and process emotions is another broad individual difference investigated in the context of verbal irony use. These individual differences are related to empathy, theory of mind (ToM), and other ways to measure emotional processing, and evidence that these effects influence sarcasm processing has been found in research studying participants with brain lesions as well as children's development of verbal irony recognition (Olkoniemi et al., 2016).

The first study to test these individual differences was Kaakinen et al. (2014, Experiment 2), also reported in Section 3.1. After providing evidence that verbal irony was associated with more rereadings and higher processing costs (Experiment 1), Kaakinen et al. (2014) conducted a second experiment to model the role of three of the individual differences described in the previous paragraph: WMC, NFC, and self-reported sarcasm use. First, they hypothesized that higher WMC might facilitate verbal irony processing because of the need to consider both contextual and linguistic information (and, according to the SPM or GSH, compare two alternative meanings). Second, they predicted participants with higher NFC might be more inclined to enjoy any processing difficulty associated with verbal irony, and thus NFC might be related to processing differences. Finally, they predicted that individuals who used sarcasm more in their daily lives (represented through higher self-reported sarcasm use) would be more apt at recognizing and processing verbal irony. Their results found no effects for self-reported sarcasm use or for NFC. Moreover, while they did find effects for WMC, these effects were relatively small and suggested that participants with higher WMC were associated with a higher probability to reread the ironic (vs. literal) uses of the target utterances during the first reading of the target utterances. At first glance this may seem like higher WMC participants encountered greater processing difficulty, but Kaakinen et al. (2014) argued this effect suggested higher WMC participants were quicker at recognizing the verbal irony and thus quicker to engage in necessary rereading during their first (rather than second, etc.) encounter with the target utterance. As such, higher WMC did appear to be associated with a greater ability to recognize and process verbal irony.

Work from the same lab continued to probe the effects of WMC and NFC during verbal irony processing as well as individual differences in emotional processing. Olkoniemi et al. (2016) examined the role of WMC, NFC, and emotional processing ability during the processing of both ironic and metaphorical utterances. Participants read stories which biased target utterances to be unfamiliar uses of irony, metaphor, or literal meaning. For example, the target utterance "well, you're hungry today!" was ironic in a context in which a character ate very little but was metaphorical in a context in which a character was described as wanting to win a soccer match. Results matched with Kaakinen et al. (2014) in that they found no effect for NFC on the processing of ironic uses of the utterances (although an effect was observed for metaphorical uses). There were several effects for WMC and emotional processing ability on the processing of ironic uses. In first pass readings, participants with higher WMC exhibited a greater tendency to reread the ironic (vs. literal) utterances as the experiment proceeded, whereas those with lower WMC tended to reread the ironic uses less as the experiment proceeded. This finding was interpreted in the same manner as Kaakinen et al. (2014), in that readers with higher WMC were able to more quickly recognize the sarcastic meanings, which needed to be reconciled via rereading. There was also an effect for emotional processing, operationalized as scores on the Iowa Gambling Test (IGT) in which higher scores represent a greater tendency to integrate emotional information when making decision. Participants with lower IGT were more likely to look back to the critical context when reading ironic (vs. literal) uses of the utterances, suggesting that a decreased tendency to integrate emotional information into cognitive decision-making may have increased the difficulty associated with processing sarcasm. The emotional information from the story context would be part of the pragmatic information thought to be necessary to interpret sarcasm, and thus this finding does highlight the role of such pragmatic information during the processing of verbal irony. As such, the results from this study replicated the findings that higher WMC might benefit irony processing, but also that a better ability to include emotional information during cognitive processing increased the ability to infer an ironic interpretation.

Olkoniemi et al. (2018) used the same material from the Olkoniemi et al. (2016), but adjusted the presentation format using masking methods. This meant the texts were initially presented as masks, with an *x* used to initially represent each letter character of each sentence. In one condition (no-mask), the text was gradually shown to participants as they read, with the preceding text left unmasked (and thus available for rereading). In the second condition, sentences were only unmasked during the first reading of the sentence, preventing the ability to look back to other portions of the text. The reason for this manipulation was to test the hypothesis that reexamining portions of the text context was a necessary function of sarcasm processing and comprehension. Their main findings indicated that the masking condition had no direct effect on sarcasm comprehension, and that readers developed task strategies to account for the masked text in the mask condition, such as spending more time reading each sentence.

Aside from their masked text manipulation, Olkoniemi et al. (2018) also gathered more measures of WMC (both verbal and spatial) and emotional processing (both immediate and inferential) when compared to Olkoniemi et al. (2016). There were effects for both of these individual differences. Readers with lower spatial WMC had longer first pass rereading times and were less likely to look back to target utterances for sarcastic (vs. literal) uses in the masked condition. In other words, readers with lower WMC relied more on rereading the target utterance when they were unable to reinspect other portions of the context, which again suggests a facilitative effect of WMC on the ability to retain information necessary for irony processing and comprehension. There was also a relationship between the measure of using emotionful information when making inferences, in that greater ability to recognize emotions was associated with fewer first pass rereadings, suggesting the recognition of emotional information facilitated verbal irony processing. Although these WMC and emotional processing measures differed from the ones used in Olkoniemi et al. (2016), these results provided further evidence that higher WMC and ability to recognize and integrate emotional information positively influences the ability to process sarcasm.

Effects for emotional measures were also reported in Olkoniemi et al. (2019), who again found participants with a decreased ability to recognize emotions were associated with a higher tendency to reread the contextual elements of the story, likely reflecting a need to search the prior context for information which was not easily gleaned during first reading. This effect however only appeared in texts in which the context was presented *before* the target utterance. Finally, Filik et al. (2018, Experiment 2) tested whether there was an association between an individual's tendency to use malicious humor and eye movements while reading sarcastic versus literal utterances. This individual difference is considered to be a personality trait and was measured using a previously validated survey to assess levels of indirect aggression among individuals. Filik et al. (2018) found, via correlational analysis, a positive relationship between the tendency to use malicious humor and eye movements which suggested sarcastic interpretations of ambiguously used utterances. This would suggest that participants who tend to use malicious humor, which may include sarcasm and other forms of verbal ridicule, also had a tendency to interpret utterances as sarcastic.

3.2.1 Key Findings from Individual Differences Research

The research reviewed in this section has highlighted two consistent effects for individual differences on verbal irony processing. First, that higher WMC is associated with a greater tendency to reread ironic uses of utterances during first pass reading times suggests higher WMC may aid in the initial recognition of verbal irony and allow for the consideration of multiple meanings during the first engagement with a target utterance. If a participant with higher WMC is thus better able to retain the contextual and pragmatic information of the story context, they would not need to return to the context and instead focus on resolving the meaning during the first go (Kaakinen et al., 2014; Olkoniemi et al., 2016). Interestingly, while this suggests multiple meanings are being considered, it also suggests contextual and pragmatic information is being used immediately, and thus whether this finding offers support for any one theory over the other may be up to the manner in which a researcher interprets the result.

The other consistent individual difference is the ability to recognize and/or process emotional information. In general, participants who can better use this information also seem better at processing sarcastic uses of target utterances, with lower reading times and less need to refer to the prior contexts. Sarcasm contains a lot of pragmatic and evaluative information, and thus it makes sense that participants better able to integrate such information may possess an advantage for sarcasm processing.

3.3 Modeling Verbal Irony Processing Using Event-Related Potentials

Just as researchers turned their gaze toward eye-tracking methods as a means to better understand the time course of verbal irony processing, neurolinguistic techniques which have become increasingly prevalent in psycholinguistic research were also employed to study verbal irony. One such method was the use of event related potentials (ERP). Two well-known ERP effects which have emerged in a number of psycholinguistic studies are the N400 and P600 effects (Kutas & Federmeier, 2011). The effects are named after their polarity (negative or positive) and the millisecond range they tend to appear within after the initial presentation of a stimulus (Kutas et al., 2006). Although the debate is certainly not settled, an extremely simplistic yet useful distinction between these two effects is that N400 waves appear to be most strongly associated with information *retrieval*, whereas P600 waves are associated with *integration* of retrieved information (Delogu et al., 2019; Kutas & Federmeier, 2011). In terms of language, the N400 effect is typically associated with lexical information (e.g., retrieving the meaning of words), whereas the P600 is typically associated with larger discursive, syntactic, or pragmatic information (e.g., integrating retrieved information to arrive at full understanding of a linguistic stimulus). During language processing, encountering words which are unexpected or otherwise poor fits for a particular context will elicit a larger N400 wave when compared to more expected words (Filik et al., 2021). On the other hand, P600 effects are observed in a similar manner for larger violations, such as syntactic or pragmatic violations (Kutas & Federmeier, 2011; Spotorno et al., 2013).

These ERP effects map somewhat fuzzily onto predictions of verbal irony processing made by the earlier theories described in Section 2. On the one hand, larger N400 or P600 effects for verbal irony likely reflect more effortful processing, which has long been taken as evidence in favor of theories like the GSH or SPM. However, alternative views might be taken. For instance, if there is initial activation of semantic meaning which is the literal meaning, one would expect a larger N400 effect when an utterance is used ironically versus literally because the "meaning" of the utterance is unexpected. However, an N400 would not necessarily disprove the direct access theory because the theory does not state that *none* of the literal meaning would be used during processing. Moreover, any P600 effects for verbal irony would suggest difficulty integrating retrieved meaning into the context, perhaps supporting the notion that context-ual information is being considered in tandem, which would align with the predictions of the direct access view. However, a P600 may not necessarily disprove the GSH or SPM because they both argue contextual information is necessary to involve a semantic incongruity! As such, one of the challenges researchers have faced is interpreting the presence or absence of these effects within the context of verbal irony processing.

3.3.1 Early ERP Studies: Verbal Irony Elicits N400 and P600 Effects

One of the earliest reports of N400 and P600 effects for verbal irony is reported in Katz et al. (2004), although details of the study are left underspecified. However, a study published soon thereafter (Cornejol et al., 2007) also reported N400 and P600 effects for verbal irony. Cornejol et al. (2007) had participants listen to target utterances biased toward a literal, ironic, or nonsensible inter-pretation, depending on the story context. The story contexts were presented auditorily, and after a 1,000 ms pause, the target utterance was presented visually for the participants, who then categorized whether the utterance was coherent or incoherent based on the story context. Half of the participants were asked to make this decision based on whether the target utterance was seman-tically compatible with the context (analytical category), while the other half (holistic category) were asked to make the decision based on whether the sentence would make sense "in real life" (Cornejol et al., 2007, p. 416). The reason for these two interpretive categories was to determine whether priming participants to use a certain interpretive strategy would affect verbal irony processing. Their results found a clear effect of analytical strategy on both the ERP measures and participant responses. Participants who were asked to think holistically were more likely to indicate the ironic utterances were congruent (78 percent) when compared to those asked to think analytically (13 percent).

Moreover, the ERP effects for each utterance use differed between the two interpretation conditions. In the holistic condition, an N400 and P600-like effect was observed for both the ironic and nonsensical utterances, whereas these effects did not appear in the analytical condition. The Cornejo et al. (2007) study thus provided empirical evidence to suggest larger interpretative processes were influencing the processing of verbal irony, something which had not been considered in prior research. At the same time, a variety of other considerations which *have* been considered in prior research were not controlled for in this study, although this is not an issue unique to this one study but rather reflects the difficulty associated with controlling for many variables in one's experimental design.

3.3.2 Later ERP Studies: Only P600 Effects for Verbal Irony?

Despite the early reports of N400 and P600 effects for verbal irony, a number of subsequent studies reported only P600 and no N400 effects (Regel et al., 2010, 2011; Spotorno et al., 2013; Weissman & Tanner, 2018). Two studies published by Regel and colleagues represent some of the first reports of this P600-only effect. In Regel et al. (2010), participants across two sessions read short stories containing comments biased to be literal or ironic and attributed to two fictional speakers. Stimuli were presented visually, with story contexts presented sentence by sentence, and target utterances presented one word at a time. In the first session, one speaker used irony 70 percent of the time, while the other was literal 70 percent of the time. In the second session, this proportion was balanced between the two speakers to be equal. The reason for doing this was to test whether participants would come to associate a tendency to use irony with one of the speakers during the first session and then bring that information with them into the second session. Their analysis found no N400 effects for verbal irony in either session, but they did find a P600 effect for trials when the less frequent ironic speaker used irony in the first session. They also found the same effect in the second session, but this time for the speaker who used irony more frequently in the first session. The lack of an N400 and presence of a P600 effect was interpreted primarily as evidence that pragmatic information was being considered when the participants were processing ironic utterances. There was also evidence of an early P200 effect, which the authors interpreted as the early integration of pragmatic information. As such, the results of Regel et al. (2010) demonstrated not just the P600 only effect for verbal irony, but also that participants were incorporating information about the fictional speakers into their interpretation of the ironic utterances, and that this information transferred across experimental sessions separated by a day's time.

In another study, Regel et al. (2011) more directly tested the predictions of the GSH, SPM, and direct access view based on the presence or absence of N400 and P600 effects. Specifically, they predicted the presence of both N400 and P600 effects would align with the predictions of the GSH and SPM, whereas the absence of both would align with the predictions of the direct access view. In addition to these predictions, they also tested the role of an ironic tone of voice, modulated through prosody (see Section 4.1). As such, participants listened to stories with target utterances biased toward an ironic or literal meaning, half of which were spoken using an ironic tone of voice. Their results found no effects for ironic tone of voice, and also no N400 effects for verbal irony. They did however report a P600 effect for verbal irony, and these effects were replicated across a second version of the study designed to control for task strategies which may have elicited the P600. The presence of the P600 effect (and other early positive wavelengths) was again interpreted as evidence that contextual and pragmatic information was being incorporated during the processing of the target utterances. This effect, combined with the lack of a N400 effect which would suggest lexical incompatibility, was taken as evidence against the predictions of the GSH and the SPM. The authors further stated these findings also did not support the direct access view because the P600 suggested additional processing difficulty, however the P600 effect seems to represent exactly what the direct access view predicts: online integration of contextual and pragmatic information during verbal irony processing.

Evidence for P600-only effects in verbal irony processing was replicated in Spotorno et al. (2013). Participants read stories designed to bias utterances toward a literal or ironic interpretation. Stories were presented one sentence at a time, with the target utterance shown one word at a time. Similar to the Regel et al. studies, ironic uses of the target utterances elicited a P600 effect when compared to the nonironic uses, with no evidence of an N400 effect. Because the P600 effect was thought to reflect more effortful processing, the authors suggested these results did not align with the predictions of the direct access view. They were also quick to note that other portions of their results suggested pragmatic information was being integrated relatively early during processing of the target utterances, which would disagree with predictions of the GSH and SPM. In the end, the authors pointed toward the constraint-satisfaction approach as the best theory fitting the results.

One final example in this section also demonstrates evidence of a P600-only effect for verbal irony. Weissman and Tanner (2018) conducted an ERP study of verbal irony processing, focusing on the role of emojis as signals for irony. They created stimuli consisting of sentences such as "the cake she made was terrible" followed by a smiling emoji ☺ (mismatch), a frowning emoji ☹ (match), or an emoji with a winking eye emoji ☺ (ironic). They also used fillers created with other emojis, such as laughing and crying faces. In Experiment 1, participants read the sentences and answered true/false questions for 33 percent of the trials (e.g., "true/false: the cake was bad"). Results included early P200 effects for ironic emojis when compared to matching (i.e., literal) emojis, as well as P600 effects for participants who responded to the true/false questions in a manner which indicated they interpreted the winky emoji as irony. However, an additional finding was that most participants did not answer the true/false questions in a manner congruent with an ironic interpretation. As such the study was repeated, with an additional instruction to participants that some of the stimuli used in the experiment would be sarcastic (Experiment 2). This manipulation had the intended effect in that participant responses in Experiment 2 were more indicative of ironic interpretations. Moreover, the same ERP effects emerged: an early P200 effect for winking emojis and a P600 effect for participants who indicated they interpreted the winky emojis as ironic. A final experiment (Experiment 3) was conducted in which the frowning emoji became the match condition, while the smiling emoji became the mismatch condition. This was done to control for potential task recognition effects in the first two experiments, and the same P200 and P600 effects were reported.

The results from Weissman and Tanner (2018) were interpreted as evidence that verbal irony processing requires integration of pragmatic and contextual information. The authors also emphasized the early P200 effects hinted at early integration, a finding reported in prior research but to date less discussed when compared to the N400 and P600 effects. One potential issue with this study relates to the presentation of single sentences devoid of context. As should be clear to the reader by now, most studies of verbal irony tend to provide contextual scenarios which then bias an utterance toward a literal or ironic meaning, but in this case the authors relied solely on the valence of the emoji to do this work. Nonetheless, that the findings using emoji were similar to other studies suggests the emojis may have indeed provided enough pragmatic or evaluative information to trigger an ironic interpretation.

3.3.3 The Fragility of the N400

Although the research in Section 3.3.2 suggests a consistent P600 effect for verbal irony processing with no N400 effect, yet another set of ERP studies reported N400 effects for verbal irony. The primary difference is that studies showing N400 effects have usually manipulated some other aspect of the study so that verbal irony is interacted with another source of information or language condition. Recall that the Cornejol et al. (2007) study which reported N400 effects also included an additional condition: differences in analytical strategies. Other studies also included additional variables, such as the Filik et al. (2014) study testing familiar and unfamiliar ironies explained in Section 3.1.3, which included a second experiment using ERP instead of eye-tracking methods. Their results did contain an N400 effect, but only for the unfamiliar ironies, which would suggest that familiarity may have been an overlooked factor in other ERP studies which did not report N400 effects. The Filik et al. (2014) study also reported a P600 effect for both familiar and unfamiliar ironies, further attesting to the notion that verbal irony processing does involve the integration of contextual and pragmatic information, even when they are familiar.

Two other studies provide additional evidence that the N400 might appear, but only in the right circumstances. Caffarra et al. (2019) used ironic and literal stimuli orally presented in Spanish, half of which was recorded by a native speaker of Spanish, and the other half of which was recorded by a second-language speaker of Spanish. The stimuli were further controlled so that some of the ironies were positive (e.g., saying "you're broke" to someone who won the lottery) and some were negative (e.g., saying "you're rich" to someone who had no money). Participants were all native speakers of Spanish, and thus would associate the recordings not spoken by the native Spanish speaker as foreign-accented Spanish. Caffarra et al. (2019) found a P600 effect similar to prior research, but also an N400 effect for ironies spoken by the native Spanish speaker in the positive contexts. One explanation for this effect is that positive uses of irony are less prototypical than negative uses (e.g., being sarcastic), and thus this N400 may be similar to the one observed by Filik et al. (2014) for unfamiliar ironies.

In a similar motivation to Caffarra et al. (2019), Caillies et al. (2019) examined the role of affect in verbal irony processing. Specifically, they cited evidence suggesting negative sarcasm is processed quicker than positive irony (referred to as the asymmetry of affect; Clark & Gerrig, 1984). Their stimuli included short single sentences which used adjectives to describe an entity in a negative (e.g., "his son is very sad") or positive ("the audience is very pleasant") manner. The sentences were recorded by a French native speaker both with and without an ironic tone of voice (see Section 4.1). Participants listened to the recordings and answered a question after each sentence which asked whether participants felt the speaker's thoughts matched with the speaker's utterance. Their results included an N400 effect for negative statements using ironic prosody when compared to nonironic prosody, with a reverse effect found between positive statements using ironic versus nonironic prosody. Results also included a P600 effect, but only for the negative ironies. The authors interpreted these findings as evidence that additional emotional or evaluative information was being considered by participants, and less prototypical cases (i.e., positive irony) elicited an N400, whereas prototypical cases (i.e., negative irony) did not. It should however be pointed out that the stimuli in this experiment were presented devoid of any additional context, aside from the tone of voice. Much like the Weissman and Tanner (2018) emoji study, it may be the case that tone of voice was enough to bias the additional pragmatic information needed to interpret irony. However, because context plays a large role in the predictions for different theoretical models of verbal irony processing, studies such as these may need to be replicated with fuller contexts before any results can be mapped onto theories.

3.3.4 Wrapping up ERP

Although it may seem like the ERP research is somewhat fuzzy in regard to verbal irony processing, there does appear to be a consistent finding in that verbal irony appears to typically elicit a P600 effect, while there is less certainty regarding the presence of N400 effects. The P600 effect might best be taken as reflecting the larger metarepresentational inferencing which is thought to be a part of understanding verbal irony (Regel et al., 2011; Spotorno et al., 2013). The elicitation of an N400 effect in many studies seems to reflect additional manipulations to stimuli beyond a basic ironic/literal dichotomy, further illustrating the need to consider additional linguistic and contextual features when testing verbal irony processing.

One irony which exists for some of these ERP studies is that target utterances were presented one word at a time, likely as a means to properly isolate ERP waves on specific portions of the target utterances (and usually the final word). Recall, however, that this method of stimuli presentation was criticized by proponents of eye tracking because it lacks ecological validity for reading processes. In addition, other ERP studies have used stimuli which are linguistically devoid of context, which may have prompted participants to focus more on linguistic features in the absence of contextual information.

Perhaps somewhat frustratingly for researchers attempting to prove one theory over another, the evidence demonstrating that the brain responds differently to verbal irony versus nonironic equivalents does little to clarify whether qualitatively different processes are in play during verbal irony processing or how the literal versus ironic meanings may be interacting. However, the consistent P600 effects do continue to suggest information beyond the lexical level is integrated during the time course of verbal irony processing, and it is thus not surprising that many of these studies have taken their results as evidence for the constraint-satisfaction approach toward verbal irony.

4 Ears and Minds: Additional Contextual Influences

Whether done using reading times, eye tracking, or ERP, the bulk if not all of the psycholinguistic research into verbal irony described in Sections 2 and 3 focused on the time course processing of irony as a means to establish whether verbal irony is more cognitively effortful to process when compared to a literal equivalent (or variations of the properties of irony, such as familiarity). The general answer appears to be yes, that verbal irony does require more effortful processing, whether measured through reading times, eye movements, or ERP effects. The potential reasons behind more effortful processing are typically attributed to conflicts involved during the integration of semantic information of target utterances and contextual information they appear within, usually as a means to test the predictions of the SPM, GSH, or direct access models.

As was discussed in Section 3, one of the ways in which the psycholinguistic study of verbal irony changed over the years was the emergence of studies which were less concerned with testing the specific predictions of the early psycholinguistic models introduced in Section 2. In particular, some researchers chose to continue identifying and exploring the specific contextual factors which may facilitate or hinder the processing of verbal irony. The theory which best supports such a pursuit is the parallel-constraint satisfaction approach (Katz, 2005; Pexman, 2008). Recall that this approach posits that verbal irony processing and comprehension involves a stock taking of multiple sources of information, including the semantic and syntactic properties of the utterance, any contextual and world information relevant to the utterance, and also information about the speaker and the context of communication. Information about the speaker could include demographic variables but also inferences made about a speaker's intentions. The context of communication can provide information about discourse expectations, tone of voice, and elicit specific emotional and pragmatic reactions depending on the configuration of the interlocutors. According to the constraint-satisfaction approach, all information relevant to an utterance is processed simultaneously through a connectionist, probabilistic network, building toward the activation of whichever type of meaning (ironic, literal, metaphorical, or otherwise) most suits the information available to the listener.

This section reviews two sources of contextual information which have attracted a great deal of attention: ironic tone of voice and ToM.

4.1 The Sounds of Irony

While a good portion of the psycholinguistic literature has presented ironic utterances as written text, plenty of studies have used audio stimuli. By using text stimuli, acoustic features of verbal irony must be supplied by the participants when reading, which raises another potential variable to be considered in the study of verbal irony (i.e., acoustic properties of sarcasm). As such, it is important to consider whether there does exist a so-called ironic tone of voice. Colloquially, an ironic tone of voice is commonly associated with prosodic or intonational patterns, which may include exaggerated pitch and/or deadpan delivery. This has led some researchers to first establish whether an ironic tone of voice exists, and if so, whether acoustic properties of irony influence online processing.

4.1.1 An Ironic Tone of Voice?

Attardo et al. (2003) investigated the intonational properties of spoken ironies via an examination of ironic utterances taken from American comedy sitcoms. They reported that different intonational patterns were associated with irony and sarcasm and identified three main categories: within-statement contrast (e.g., initial high pitch followed by lower pitch), compressed pitch pattern (i.e., flat, deadpan intonation), and pronounced pitch accents (e.g., exaggerated pitch placed on multiple words/syllables in an utterance). The main function of these patterns, they argued, was to signal a contrast to the listener, but no single pitch range or intonational pattern could be described as *the* ironic tone of voice.

The prosodic properties of an ironic tone of voice have been further investigated via a production study, where native English speakers were asked to produce utterances biased to be sarcastic, humorous, or sincere (Cheang & Pell, 2008). The authors compared the pitch frequency and speech rate among these three types, finding that sarcasm was marked by a significantly lower fundamental frequency (F0) with very little variation, which reflects the deadpan, flat intonation style of stereotypical descriptions of sarcastic speech. A similar study asked participants to speak sentences reflecting negative or positive assessments in either a teasing, sarcastic, nice, or mean manner (Mauchand et al., 2018). These results indicated that prosodic features distinguished between sarcasm and niceness for the positive sentences, in that sarcasm was marked by lower variations in pitch, but no other acoustic features were found to be significant. Moreover, there is some evidence to suggest that while prosodic features are used as cues to irony and sarcasm in languages other than English and across English varieties, these features are not necessarily used in the same way as English (Cheang & Pell, 2009; Chen & Boves, 2018; Li et al., 2020; Lœvenbruck et al., 2013).

As such, these studies indicate that there are prosodic features which distinguish sarcasm and verbal irony from other forms of speech. However, both descriptive and statistical analyses indicate these features are not stable enough to identify a single ironic tone of voice, but instead suggest speakers have a range of prosodic strategies which can be used to mark an ironic intention (Voyer & Techentin, 2010).

4.1.2 Does Prosody Influence Irony Processing?

Some of the ERP studies reviewed in Section 3 employed auditory stimuli, and in turn studied whether the effects of prosody influenced sarcasm processing. The results suggest somewhat mixed effects for prosody. For instance, Regel et al. (2011) found no clear influence of prosody on ERP effects, while Caillies et al. (2019) did find effects. In a similar study to Caillies et al. (2019), Thompson et al. (2021) conducted an ERP study with prosody across two experiments but also used stimuli which provided contextual information both before and after the target utterances. All literal utterances were recorded using a natural tone of voice, whereas the ironic utterances were all recorded with either a natural or an ironic tone of voice. The context contained additional information about either the target or the speaker of the irony. Specifically, information indicated whether the target was amused (Experiment 1) or hurt (Experiment 2) by the target utterances (e.g., "when George heard the comment, he was amused/hurt"), or whether the speaker hoped the target was amused/hurt (e.g., "Jerry hoped George would hear the comment and be amused/hurt"). The authors included this contextual information as a means to control for expected or unexpected emotions associated with sarcasm, in that hurtful feelings were predicted to be more expected than amused feelings. The amused/hurt words appeared as the final words in each sentence and ERP data was collected for both the entire utterance and the critical words. While Thompson et al. (2021) found P600 effects between speaker and target perspectives for the amused condition, in that there was stronger P600 for target perspectives (Experiment 1), they found no significant results for this difference in the hurt condition (Experiment 2). The authors interpreted this interaction to support their predictions that sarcasm would be associated with hurtful feelings from both the target and speaker points of view, and this expectation explained why there was no P600 effect in the hurtful condition. Conversely, the amusement associated with sarcasm in the amused condition was less expected, and thus a P600 wave suggested a more difficult integration of the sarcasm with the other contextual information. Though not the same as the N400, their results also demonstrated early negative ERP effects (i.e., N200) for irony delivered with ironic prosody, suggesting the prosodic features were being interpreted quickly and may have aided in the ultimate interpretation of an ironic utterance. In this case, their results were similar in nature to the findings of Caillies et al. (2019), suggesting intonation facilitated the early recognition of spoken irony.

In addition, an ERP study by Mauchand et al. (2021) asked participants to listen to single sentences with either positive or negative evaluation (e.g., "you are such a great/horrible cook") and spoken with either a neutral or ironic prosody. After hearing each sentence, participants were asked to rate the friendliness of the speaker on a five-point scale. They compared ERP effects at the onset of the stimuli to ERP effects occurring during the critical word, finding significant effects for prosody. In short, prosody provided early information about the speaker's stance, which then interacted with the meaning of the utterance to generate inferences about the speaker's intentions. Mauchand et al. (2021) thus argued prosody was being used to predict speaker's intentions even before hearing the utterance, which would suggest rapid integration processes of all relevant sources of information, in line with the constraint-satisfaction view.

Rivière et al. (2018) sought to test the relative weight of prosodic cues in irony recognition against another irony cue: contextual incongruity. Participants listened to story contexts which ended in target utterances that represented different degrees of incongruity with the prior context. For example, the target utterance "Christine is a clever student" is congruous with a context in which Christine studied for one day and received full marks, is slightly incongruous with a context where she studied for two days and received a 60 percent mark, and is highly incongruous in a context where she hardly studied and received a 20 percent mark. The degree of contextual incongruity thus biased a target utterance toward a sarcastic or literal use. Additionally, the target statements were recorded with both an ironic and neutral prosody. Participants were asked to listen to each story and decide, as quickly as possible, whether or not the story was ironic. In order to derive a metric indicating reliance on prosodic cues, the authors used cluster analysis to divide participants into two groups depending upon their answers to target items in the weak contextual incongruity category, where prosody would arguably be a stronger effect. Participants who had fewer answers indicating the stories were ironic in the weak contextual incongruity category were thought to rely less on prosody, and were classified as the PROSODY− group, whereas the other participants were classified as the PROSODY+ group. These two groups were then compared across all contextual conditions. Results indicated that while the PROSODY− group had a higher incidence of indicating target utterances were ironic across all conditions, this effect was seen most strongly in the weak incongruity condition spoken with neutral prosody. Conversely, PROSODY+ participants did not detect irony in the weak incongruity context when no prosodic markers were present.

There was also a main effect for reaction times, in that the PROSODY− group made their decisions significantly faster than the PROSODY+. As such, the main contribution from this study is that it provides evidence indicating individuals differ in the relative weight they place on prosodic versus contextual cues, with some individuals placing a stronger emphasis on the role of prosody during sarcasm use. If this effect is generalizable, it means that the integration of prosodic information is another individual difference which may impact the way that verbal irony is recognized, processed, and comprehended.

4.1.3 Other Prosodic Features

Matsui et al. (2016) conducted a study using fMRI to further test the role of prosody during sarcasm comprehension in Japanese. They created a series of visual stories depicting a parent having a conversation with a child. Each story biased a target utterance spoken by the parent toward a sarcastic or literal use, depending on the prior actions of the child. Also, target utterances were spoken with either negative or affective prosody. Crucially, the authors distinguished this affective prosody from the notion of an ironic tone of voice, and as such more directly investigated attitudinal effects present in the acoustic properties of the target utterances. Participants were presented with stimuli which included visual depictions of the stories, with the sentences presented as text while speakers listened to a voice read the text. Participants answered whether the target utterance in each story was sincere or not. Results indicated that prosody facilitated sarcasm recognition, in that target utterances using positive prosody following negative behavior (i.e., sarcasm) were seen to be more sarcastic than sincere criticism. The fMRI results indicated that the interaction among prosody, context, and target utterance could be pinpointed to a specific region of the brain (the left inferior frontal gyrus) thought to be active during resolution of conflicting sources of information, which had also been reported in some prior fMRI studies (Matsui et al., 2016). As such, the results from this study provide further evidence that prosody (in this case, affective tone) is among the features which influence the online processing of verbal irony.

Aside from prosody and intonational cues associated with verbal irony of affective stances, another acoustic feature which has been recently explored is the role of foreign accent on verbal irony processing and comprehension. Recall the Caffarra et al. (2019) ERP study, which reported N400 effects for ironic praise when spoken by a native versus foreign accent. Although a prior offline study had indicated participants rated foreign-accented ironic praise as significantly less ironic when compared to native accents (Caffarra et al., 2018), the ERP results suggested online processing influences (i.e., N400 effects) for less prototypical irony (i.e., ironic praise) when spoken in a native accent, with no effects between irony type for foreign accents. Caffarra et al. (2019) interpreted these effects as evidence that information about the speakers indexed through accents were being integrated during processing, which they indicated aligned with the predictions of the constraint-satisfaction approach.

4.1.4 Sound Off

In sum, while there is no single unified ironic tone of voice, acoustic properties appear to be one cue hearers across languages attend to when interpreting verbal irony. Moreover, these features appear to serve as early cues to some, but not all hearers that the speaker is at least intending to be ironic. As such these studies do provide some evidence indicating how, at least in the case of spoken ironies, acoustic properties are one constraint which can be incorporated swiftly during processing, which further aligns with the predictions of the constraint-satisfaction account.

4.2 Theory of Mind and Verbal Irony

The ability to infer speaker intentions is another key variable which has been explored in the context of verbal irony processing. In particular, an overarching theory which has united these studies is a concept known as theory of mind (ToM). Theory of mind is the ability to understand one's own perspectives and beliefs as well as the ability to infer other people's beliefs and subsequent behavior based upon their beliefs (Frith & Frith, 2005). Because understanding verbal irony is thought to require metarepresentational inferences about a speaker and other aspects of the contextual situation associated with the irony (Colston & Gibbs, 2002), it is not surprising that researchers have sought to establish links between ToM and the ability to process and comprehend verbal irony. Developmental studies, for instance, have suggested that children do not develop a sense of irony until roughly the ages of five to six, in part because it is not until this time that children develop a ToM (Glenwright & Pexman, 2010).

4.2.1 fMRI Studies of Verbal Irony and Theory of Mind

Research exploring ToM outside the context of verbal irony processing has used fMRI technology to identify a network of brain regions thought to be specific to ToM activation (Gallagher & Frith, 2003). These regions include areas of the right and left temporal–parietal junctions, the medial prefrontal cortex, and the precuneus (Spotorno et al., 2012). As such, verbal irony researchers have been able to investigate whether these same regions are active during the processing of verbal irony. The general logic of doing so is that if verbal irony processing excites regions of the brain associated with ToM to a greater extent than literal uses, this would be evidence that ToM is a specific component of verbal irony processing (Noveck, 2018).

Early fMRI research into verbal irony proceeded at the same time (or before) the reading time, eye tracking, and ERP studies discussed in Sections 2, 3, and 4. In general, these fMRI studies did report differences in brain activation for sarcasm versus literal equivalents (Uchiyama et al., 2006), as well as between sarcasm and other figurative language, such as metaphor (Eviatar & Just, 2006; Uchiyama et al., 2012). However, a study published in 2012 pointed out that none of the fMRI research into verbal irony processing had provided any direct links between verbal irony processing and established regions of the brain associated with ToM (Spotorno et al., 2012). One potential reason for this lack of evidence was thought to be attributed to the stimuli and other methodological concerns raised by Spotorno et al. (2012), and thus they designed a study intending to more precisely test the hypothesis using more appropriate stimuli. To do so, they presented participants with stories including target utterances biased toward a literal or sarcastic interpretation, along with an additional set of stories in negative contexts which were not sarcastic (to control for task strategies based on associating negative contexts with sarcasm use). Stories were presented one line at a time, and participants answered a comprehension question about each story which was not associated with the ironic or literal meaning. Their results included three main findings: ironic uses of the utterances took more time to read than literal uses, that ToM regions of the brain (right and left temporal–parietal junctions, the medial prefrontal cortex, and the precuneus) were active for ironic but not literal uses, and that ToM regions of the brain were coactivated with language processing regions (left inferior frontal gyrus) during verbal irony processing. These results were taken as concrete evidence providing a link between irony and ToM because language processing regions of the brain were coactivated with ToM for verbal irony but not for the nonironic uses.

Since the Spotorno et al. (2012) study, several other fMRI studies have presented results which suggest that regions of the brain associated with ToM are more active during verbal irony processing (Akimoto et al., 2014; Bosco et al., 2017; Filik et al., 2019; Obert et al., 2016). Among these studies, Akimoto et al. (2014) was directly motivated by the predictions of the constraint-satisfaction model (Pexman, 2008). Participants were presented with stimuli in which they took on the role of a character referred to as "you" in each story. The stories were also presented visually, with a small avatar representing "you," and two pictures to represent other characters in the situation. Each story contained an introduction in which the avatar representing "you" agreed to do something with one of the other two characters, while the second character did something else (e.g., one character and "you" agree to ski down an advanced slope, while the other character chooses the beginner route). This agreement created the same expectation toward "you" from *both* characters (e.g., that "you" can manage to ski down an advanced slope). Afterward, text appeared summarizing "your" subsequent actions as either meeting that expectation (e.g., "you" ski down well) or failing to meet that expectation (e.g., "you" got scared and skied poorly, but still made it to the bottom). Finally, one of the two characters then said something to "you" (e.g., "you are a good skier"), which was expected to be interpreted as sarcastic or literal. Crucially, the sarcastic (failed expectations) or literal (met expectations) interpretations would only be present when the character that stayed with "you" made the utterance because only they would be aware of whether "you" met or failed to meet the expectation (interested readers may want to refer directly to figure 1 in Akimoto et al. (2014) for a clear depiction of this stimulus). For the other character, their utterance in the failed expectation condition would be interpreted from their point of view as literal, despite the potential irony which could arise from the statement (the authors labeled this as the *incongruity* condition). As such, the point of view of the speaker was integral for understanding irony.

Participants proceeded through these stories, answering a dummy task at the end of each story. Afterward, they were presented with the same situation and asked to indicate the intentions of the speaker as ironic or literal, as well as rate the target utterances for irony, humor, and negative emotions. The authors analyzed these ratings in tandem with the fMRI measures. One of the key results was that participants exhibited high accuracy when asked to attribute the intentions of the unaware character whose utterance might result in unintentional irony. In other words, the participants took into account the intentions of the speaker when determining if the utterance was ironic or literal. Their results included activation of brain regions associated with ToM, such as the medial prefrontal cortex, but also results indicating that bran regions *not* associated with ToM (right anterior superior temporal gyrus) were associated with the social, conceptual knowledge of irony. As such, this study provided evidence that ToM was important for irony processing, while also identifying specific regions for irony itself.

The results from these studies suggest that specific regions of the brain associated with ToM are active during the processing of verbal irony, in turn suggesting mentalizing or perspective taking is a crucial component of understanding verbal irony. In contrast to many prior studies which have sought to find out whether verbal irony takes longer to process than nonironic equivalents, these studies provide potential explanations for *why* a processing difference might exist.

4.2.2 Other ToM Studies

In a bit of a shocking departure from the fMRI experiments, Baptista et al. (2018) used electrical stimulation methods to directly excite or inhibit the medial prefrontal cortex of participants. By purposefully activating or blocking the medial prefrontal cortex, Baptista et al. (2018) were able to directly manipulate one of the key regions associated with ToM use. In the study, participants were assigned to one of three conditions: ToM activation, ToM blocking, or a sham condition in which the electrical wave was turned off after 20 seconds. For the activation or blocking conditions, electrical stimulation was conducted for 20 minutes. Afterward participants then participated in an ERP study, where they were shown slides providing some contextual information (e.g., "the man's car"), and then shown an image (e.g., a picture of a man in a very small car), and then shown a written statement biased to be literal or ironic depending on the prior context (e.g., "how spacious"). Participants were asked to indicate whether the target utterances were ironic or literal. N400 effects for verbal irony were reported, but only for participants in the conditions which inhibited their medial prefrontal cortex or in the sham condition which did not use any electrical stimulation. Although there are implications for this study in terms of the ERP results presented in Section 3, the results from this study are perhaps most interesting for probing the relationship between verbal irony and ToM, because they suggested higher ToM facilitated irony processing. However, the stimuli were presented with very little context, and the participants were explicitly asked to judge if the stimuli were ironic or literal, which likely increased the chances for N400 effects to emerge.

Differences in ToM have been posited as an alternative explanation for why some early processing studies of verbal irony, such as those reviewed in Sections 2 and 3, reported more effortful processing for ironic as compared to literal uses of target utterances (Spotorno & Noveck, 2014). To test this notion, Spotorno and Noveck (2014) returned to the stimuli used in Spotorno et al. (2012), which demonstrated fMRI evidence for the role of ToM during verbal irony processing. However, instead of using fMRI, the 2014 study employed a measure of sentence reading times. In Experiment 1, they used the same stimuli as the 2012 study, which included ironic, literal, and decoy texts. They also measured the social skills of participants as a means to operationalize preexisting ability to mentalize. Participants read target stories sentence by sentence in a self-paced manner. Results from Experiment 1 showed reading times for target and spillover utterances were significantly longer for ironic (vs. literal) uses of sentences, providing evidence of the typical processing costs seen for verbal irony in the literature. Moreover, there was no significant relationship between social skills and text processing. This null result for social skills was explained as expected because the decoy stories (which were negative contexts but not ironic) did not allow participants to attribute a negative attitude with verbal irony use, and thus not tap into social skills reflecting ToM ability.

Spotorno and Noveck (2014) then repeated Experiment 1 but without the decoy stories, with the expectation that the stimuli would now allow participants with higher ToM ability to associate negative contexts with ironic intent. The Experiment 2 results confirmed this expectation, because ironic target utterances were read slower than literal uses, but only during the first half of the experiment. Moreover, there was no correlation between their measure of ToM and reading behavior during the first half of the experiment, but there was a significant negative relationship between those with higher ToM ability and differences in reading times. Specifically, a higher ToM ability was associated with decreased differences in reading times between ironic and literal uses during the second half of the experiment. The researchers interpreted these results to suggest that in the absence of negative decoy stories, participants with higher ToM ability were able to create an association between the negative contexts and irony, whereas those with lower ToM ability were less able to do so. As such, ToM ability appeared to modulate differences in reading times between ironic and literal uses of the same target utterances, which the authors argued best aligned with the predictions of the parallel-constraint approach.

4.3 Satisfied?

Based on the studies reviewed in this section as well as others, there is a growing body of studies which seek to interpret their results in light of the constraint-satisfaction approach to verbal irony. This may reflect the flexibility of the approach and its ability to more easily integrate the range of new findings, many of which have been made possible through the application of methods beyond reading times, such as eye tracking, ERP, and fMRI. However, as several researchers have pointed out, the constraint-satisfaction approach fails to provide specific predictions beyond the contention that irony processing is a result of probabilistic reconciliation of multiple sources of information (e.g., Rothermich et al., 2021; Ţurcan & Filik, 2017). It seems likely then to expect future developments or modifications of the parallel-constraint view, alongside continued methical innovation, both of which are healthy steps forward in order to develop a better understanding of verbal irony processing.

5 Future Directions

While the psycholinguistic research into verbal irony processing appears to have matured, there are still a number of potential future areas of research. As has been evident throughout, the vast majority of studies have focused primarily on sarcasm, which represents but a single type of irony. Future studies could test hyperbole, understatement, rhetorical questions, and other means of eliciting ironic meaning. Doing so would help determine whether the results from prior research are specific to sarcasm or more general to all members of the irony family. Because sarcasm conveys negative attitudinal meaning, testing other forms of irony that lack this pragmatic information may help further unpack the nature of ironic meaning. Aside from this, there are a number of other potential future directions in this field. The following sections review some possibilities.

5.1 Innovation in Modeling Contexts of Verbal Irony

Based on the current trajectory, it seems likely future researchers will continue to expand upon the predictions of the constraint-satisfaction approach. The predictions from constraint-satisfaction are appealing because they are inclusive in regard to the types of information which can be considered during the processing of verbal irony (or any language form). These same predictions can be intimidating however, particularly when trying to model the wide range of potential linguistic and contextual variables available to a listener. This challenge has been present since the early psycholinguistic studies of verbal irony and will likely continue to persist in future studies.

One useful resource which may account for a greater number of these contextual variables was used in a recent eye-tracking study of verbal irony (Rothermich et al., 2021). In this study, the researchers used short videos from the Relational Inference in Social Communication (RISC) database (Rothermich & Pell, 2015). The videos included actors carrying out short dialogues intended to be literal, sarcastic, humorous, and more. Rothermich et al. (2021) tracked participants' eye movements while watching these stories, finding significant differences in how long participants fixated on faces for ironic versus literal situations, suggesting that participants were attending to nonverbal cues while resolving ironic meaning, which would support predictions of the constraint-satisfaction model.

Another innovative study developed a method to better involve participants in the context of irony (Kowatch et al., 2013). These researchers modified the visual world paradigm, where eye movements are tracked across various objects in a scene. In their stimuli, participants listened to a puppet utter different preferences for certain food items using ironic criticism (e.g., "I just love apples" uttered with a mocking, negative tone), literal criticism (e.g., "I just hate apples"), or literal compliment (e.g., "I just love apples" in a neutral tone). In each trial, two plastic replicas of food were placed in front of the participants, one of which was named in the utterance. The participants' task was to select the food item the puppet actually wanted to eat by placing the plastic food replica into a shopping cart. The researchers recorded which objects the participants looked at during each trial, as well as how long it took participants to make each decision. The key findings from this study were that no significant differences were found for reaction times between ironic and literal criticisms, and that participants looked toward the correct choice first when hearing ironic utterances (suggesting immediate access of the ironic intentions). The primary contribution of this study was methodological innovation in that participants were asked to respond to the irony in a way that reflected correct or incorrect interpretation without directly asking participants to indicate if something was sarcastic. Another improvement was that the valence of the ironic and nonironic utterances was matched (i.e., both were negative), allowing for better comparison that also took into account pragmatic meaning.

5.2 Multilingual Verbal Irony Processing

Another avenue for future research is a consideration of multilingual knowledge. Although the majority of the psycholinguistic literature investigating verbal irony production has been published in English, the actual experiments have been conducted using stimuli from a variety of different languages, including English, Finnish, French, German, Hebrew, Japanese, Portuguese, Spanish, and likely more. This testing of irony in different languages has the benefit of further suggesting that irony and sarcasm are universal linguistic traits and helps address concerns that theoretical findings regarding the processing of verbal irony may be conflated with the linguistic features of any one particular language. That being said, a solid consideration for future research is testing the processing of verbal irony in a second, third, or otherwise additional language. Work in this area has already begun in terms of multilingual processing of multiple types of figurative language (e.g., Heredia & Cieślicka, 2015).

One caution which should be taken in multilingual verbal irony research is that a language learner with lower second-language proficiency is likely to rely more heavily on bottom-up lexical decoding, which may in turn lead to interpretations that processing of irony for these learners requires the initial processing of literal meaning. As such, this research should take care to clearly separate effects of second-language lexical and reading proficiency from processing of ironic meaning. Moreover, it is very likely that learning how to be ironic in an additional language involves learning the pragmatic uses, which is among the latest stages of attaining proficiency in an additional language. It is thus important for researchers in this area to consider both the semantic *and* pragmatic aptitude of their participants, otherwise this research may inadvertently perpetuate a modular view of verbal irony processing. Researchers interested in investigating multilingual figurative language processing should thus generate clear predictions for their studies based on current first language understandings of figurative language in order to avoid pitfalls such as hyper focusing on semantic but not pragmatic aspects of the stimuli.

5.3 Assessing Verbal Irony Comprehension

It is crucial to connect processing data with comprehension data (Ferreira & Yang, 2019), especially in light of evidence that the increased processing effort associated with verbal irony is no guarantee that ironic meaning will be successfully comprehended (Olkoniemi et al., 2018). The existing research has included a variety of means for assessing irony comprehension, including lexical decision tasks using words thought to relate to literal or ironic meaning, memory tasks or paraphrase judgments, or true/false questions about a character's state of mind. Recent studies have employed a comprehension check where participants are asked to identify if a target utterance is ironic, literal, or otherwise. While this might provide a convenient assessment of comprehension accuracy, it may also reduce the ecological validity of the task and cause participants to engage in strategic behavior not reflective of authentic language use. Moreover, the identification of an utterance as ironic or otherwise does not necessarily mean a participant has comprehended the *meaning* of the utterance – which for sarcasm and irony includes a range of possible semantic and pragmatic information.

Studies such as Kowatch et al. (2013), where participants indicated their answers through physical action and engagement with the ironic utterances, provide an alternative and innovative method for assessing verbal irony comprehension. Another possibility may be to implement a form of the false memory tests suggested by Katz and Reid (2020) as a method for assessing comprehension of conceptual metaphor. Studies may also want to consider more than one measure of comprehension as a means to triangulate their findings.

The literature related to discourse processing *in general* is also a seemingly underutilized field for developing models of verbal irony comprehension.

Specifically, theories of discourse comprehension posit that readers construct a mental model while reading and have tracked the various ways this model interacts with different sources of information to make inferences and other types of comprehension (Kendeou & O'Brien, 2018; McNamara & Magliano, 2009). Because verbal irony is an inferential process, it may be the case that existing models of discourse comprehension as well as specific predictions about inferencing could be mapped to incorporate verbal irony.

Another tack is to analyze what happens when participants *do not* understand ironic meaning. In some cases, researchers discard response to ironic stimuli which are deemed inaccurate. But it also may be the case that participants fail to agree a stimulus is ironic for multiple interesting reasons, ranging from semantic processing to disagreement with the speaker's intentions. As studies of failed humor have demonstrated (Bell, 2015), looking at why pragmatic phenomena do *not* work can be equally as fruitful.

5.4 Verbal Irony Production

As I have argued elsewhere, almost all of the psycholinguistic studies have focused on the online processing of verbal irony from the listener's point of view (Skalicky, 2020). A largely untapped area can be seen through investigations of the time course of verbal irony *production*. In my study (Skalicky, 2020), I was interested in assessing differences related to creativity of speaker production of sarcasm, but I also measured production times of the sarcasms as well as cognitive individual differences such as WMC and NFC. I used a set of nine comics depicting different amounts of contextual information and asked my participants to think of something sarcastic they would say, were they in those situations.

The comics differed in that the first one-third contained two speakers on a desert island with no prior speech and very few objects in the scene (these were adapted *Bizarro!* one-panel comics), the second one-third of the comics contained two speakers after an event (e.g., a vase is broken), with one of the speakers saying something (e.g., "that was my mother's favorite vase!"). The final one-third contained two speakers across multiple panes, in which a speaker first initiated an expectation (e.g., a boy brags to a girl that he can beat her in a race), which is then violated (e.g., the boy loses the race). As such, the different comics provided my participants with varying degrees of contextual and linguistic echoes to draw from when producing their sarcasms. My results indicated that participants produced more similar answers as a function of *richer* context availability, and also that these answers were rated as *less* creative by human raters. This suggests that in a context-rich environment, there were more obvious routes toward making sarcasm, especially when there was a prior utterance which could be echoed. Conversely, the most creative sarcasms were produced in response to the comics with virtually no context (i.e., the desert island comics). In these situations, participants were tasked with inventing both contextual information *and* a sarcastic utterance, further evincing the strong ties between verbal irony and context. Alongside these effects was a main effect of production time – sarcastic responses which took longer to produce were associated with significantly higher perceptions of creativity. I argued that one interpretation of this effect is that participants who spent more time were further considering the range of possible sarcastic replies which fit still fit within the context, but it could also reflect the recruitment of background knowledge and other cognitive resources.

I recognize that my study is not the only study of verbal irony production. For instance Campbell and Katz (2012) asked participants to create *contexts* which would bias a decontextualized utterance toward sarcastic or literal meanings. My point here is primarily to encourage more research focusing specifically on the time course of irony production, which when matched with participant individual differences and applied to different testing paradigms may reveal the other side of the coin in verbal irony: sarcasm from the speaker's point of view.

5.5 Satire

Satire and satirical discourse is strongly associated with verbal irony yet has received almost no attention from psycholinguists (Simpson, 2003; Skalicky, 2019). Perhaps the main difference between satirical discourse and the types of verbal irony presented in this Element (i.e., mainly sarcasm) is that satirical discourse creates an additional irony at a discursive level – one which is cocreated between a satirist and reader and is highly prone to failure (Simpson, 2003). The satirical message is thus more difficult to define or summarize when compared to ironic meaning (which itself can elude easy description), making it difficult if not impossible to construct and compare satirical and nonsatirical equivalents.

A question of interest then is whether satirical discourse processing is similar to verbal irony processing. I have provided some preliminary answers to this question. In one study, I measured reading times for satirical headlines from *The Onion* (e.g., *North Korea Successfully Harvests Wheat in Show of Growing Strength*) and nonsatirical headlines from *The New York Times* (e.g., *North Korean Propaganda Video Shows Nuclear Strike On American Capital*), which were matched on various lexical features but could not be matched for equivalent meanings (Skalicky & Crossley, 2019). Results showed that, on their own, satirical headlines were read on average slower than nonsatirical head-lines, but that this effect was qualified by a variety of text- and speaker-level variables. Participants who scored higher on a test of general knowledge were faster at reading the satirical headlines *and* provided higher ratings of humor, suggesting these participants were better able to recognize and interpret the satirical meaning (although humor can only be taken as a proxy of satire comprehension). These results are similar to the verbal irony research in that although there was a processing cost for satirical discourse, this cost was attributed to a series of constraints beyond the semantic nature of the stimuli.

In a follow-up study, I presented participants with full satirical news texts, again from *The Onion* and another nonsatirical news site (Skalicky, 2019). In this study, I was interested in again comparing reading times but also obtaining a better understanding of whether participants comprehended the satirical meaning. As such, I asked participants to rate each text for sincerity and humor, and also to write a short description of the intended meaning of the author. Inspired by the research investigating cognitive individual differences in verbal irony processing (Kaakinen et al., 2014; Olkoniemi et al., 2016), I also measured participants' NFC. I found that participants with greater NFC spent less time reading satirical (vs. nonsatirical texts), suggesting those participants who enjoyed engaging in cognitively difficult tasks were able to process satire quicker. Recall that NFC was not shown to influence verbal irony processing, suggesting these results may be specific to satire but not verbal irony. As for the comprehension answers, I manually coded the answers into a binary classifica-tion and found that only about 32 percent of the summaries of the texts represented a recognition of a satirical meaning. Moreover, processing time was *not* associated with this variable, indicating no clear link between slower/faster reading times and satire comprehension. Variables that did influence satire comprehension were perceptions of sincerity, in that participants were much more likely to summarize satirical meaning if they also rated the text low for sincerity. This finding suggested that inferences about the author of the satirical text were crucial in comprehending the satirical message, another effect that aligns well with our understanding of ironic inferencing.

One existing challenge with measuring satire comprehension which differs from verbal irony is that the coconstructed nature of satirical meaning allows readers to construct myriad possible correct interpretations (Pfaff & Gibbs, 1997). I have continued to work on assessing satirical processing and compre-hension with sentence-by-sentence and word-by-word reading studies using modified minimally-different satirical and nonsatirical news texts (Skalicky, In press, 2022). Results from these studies continue to demonstrate a processing cost for satirical discourse, but also that satire processing and comprehension is strongly related to perceptions of the satirist, such as sincerity, and not necessarily with increased processing effort. In this sense, the processing of satire likely involves many of the same inferential processes as verbal irony, but perhaps to different degrees. As such, continued investigations of satirical discourse and other cousins of irony are one additional way to advance research in this area.

6 Conclusion: Isn't It Ironic?

There exists an overwhelming amount of published literature on verbal irony and its related forms, both within psycholinguistics and without. It is impossible to cover every perspective with equal emphasis in this Element – there is simply too much published research. As such, the goal of this Element was to introduce the reader to some of the major psycholinguistic models which have exerted strong influence over the research in this area, as well as other studies which have contributed to the development of the field over the past few decades. In doing so, I summarized key studies and questions in the field, some of which still rage on today. The organization of this Element was partially based on theory, partially based on methods, and partially based on my own personal interpretations.

I began this Element with a discussion of Alanis Morissette's famous song *Ironic*. As I mentioned in that section, most people have strong perceptions regarding what is and is not ironic, leading to disagreement, debate, and a healthy amount of research. Psycholinguistic studies provide an interesting window into this debate, one which will likely continue to glean new insight as more and more researchers echo Morissette's refrain.

I conclude with a brief reminder of perhaps the most important issue faced by past, current, and future psycholinguistic studies of verbal irony. If one were to take a tally of the studies reviewed in this Element, it seems clear that for the most part verbal irony takes longer to read or requires more effortful processing when compared to some form of literal equivalent. Yet, there exists a trove of reasons for why verbal irony sometimes requires more effort, and these reasons span well beyond a comparison of so-called literal versus ironic meanings. As such, a focus on these processing differences need not be the only way to study verbal irony through a psycholinguistic lens (see Section 4, as well as Noveck, 2018). It is undisputable that irony is part of the social experience and communicates a great deal of pragmatic information that is difficult if not impossible to replicate with so-called literal equivalents that only consider semantic meaning (Colston, 2015; Colston & Gibbs, 2021; Gibbs, 2005; Gibbs & Colston, 2012).

In this sense, figurative language, including verbal irony, does not merely represent a choice between two equal ways of saying something, but is instead a means of conveying specific pragmatic information efficiently and directly (Colston, 2015; Colston & Gibbs, 2021). As such, unpacking what irony *means* requires a consideration of this pragmatic, attitudinal, and other information: "pragmatics always matters" (Gibbs & Colston, 2020). Future psycholinguistic studies should continue to push the envelope and use stimuli which are ecologically valid and attend to these considerations.

References

Akimoto, Y., Sugiura, M., Yomogida, Y. et al. (2014). Irony comprehension: Social conceptual knowledge and emotional response: Comprehending Irony. *Human Brain Mapping, 35*(4), 1167–78. https://doi.org/10.1002/hbm.22242.

Attardo, S. (2000). Irony as relevant inappropriateness. *Journal of Pragmatics, 32*, 793–826.

Attardo, S., Eisterhold, J., Hay, J., & Poggi, I. (2003). Multimodal markers of irony and sarcasm. *Humor, 16*(2), 243–60. https://doi.org/10.1515/humr.2003.012.

Baptista, N. I., Manfredi, M., & Boggio, P. S. (2018). Medial prefrontal cortex stimulation modulates irony processing as indexed by the N400. *Social Neuroscience, 13*(4), 495–510. https://doi.org/10.1080/17470919.2017.1356744.

Bell, N. D. (2015). *We are not amused: Failed humor in interaction.* Mouton de Gruyter.

Bezuidenhout, A., & Cutting, J. C. (2002). Literal meaning, minimal propositions, and pragmatic processing. *Journal of Pragmatics, 34*(4), 433–56. https://doi.org/10.1016/S0378-2166(01)00042-X.

Bosco, F. M., Parola, A., Valentini, M. C., & Morese, R. (2017). Neural correlates underlying the comprehension of deceitful and ironic communicative intentions. *Cortex, 94*, 73–86. https://doi.org/10.1016/j.cortex.2017.06.010.

Cacioppo, J. T., Petty, R., & Kao, C. F. (1984). The efficient assessment of need for cognition. *Journal of Personality Assessment, 48*(3), 306–07.

Caffarra, S., Michell, E., & Martin, C. D. (2018). The impact of foreign accent on irony interpretation. *PLOS ONE, 13*(8), e0200939. https://doi.org/10.1371/journal.pone.0200939.

Caffarra, S., Motamed Haeri, A., Michell, E., & Martin, C. D. (2019). When is irony influenced by communicative constraints? ERP evidence supporting interactive models. *European Journal of Neuroscience, 50*(10), 3566–77. https://doi.org/10.1111/ejn.14503.

Caillies, S., Gobin, P., Obert, A. et al. (2019). Asymmetry of affect in verbal irony understanding: What about the N400 and P600 components? *Journal of Neurolinguistics, 51*, 268–77. https://doi.org/10.1016/j.jneuroling.2019.04.004.

Campbell, J. D., & Katz, A. (2012). Are there necessary conditions for inducing a sense of sarcastic irony? *Discourse Processes, 49*(6), 459–80. https://doi.org/10.1080/0163853X.2012.687863.

Cheang, H. S., & Pell, M. D. (2008). The sound of sarcasm. *Speech Communication, 50*(5), 366–81. https://doi.org/10.1016/j.specom.2007.11.003.

Cheang, H. S., & Pell, M. D. (2009). Acoustic markers of sarcasm in Cantonese and English. *The Journal of the Acoustical Society of America, 126*(3), 1394–405. https://doi.org/10.1121/1.3177275.

Chen, A., & Boves, L. (2018). What's in a word: Sounding sarcastic in British English. *Journal of the International Phonetic Association, 48*(1), 57–76. https://doi.org/10.1017/S0025100318000038.

Clark, H. H., & Gerrig, R. J. (1984). On the pretense theory of irony. *Journal of Experimental Psychology: General, 113*(1), 121–26.

Colston, H. L. (2015). *Using figurative language.* Cambridge University Press.

Colston, H. L. (2017). Irony and sarcasm. In S. Attardo (Ed.), *The Routledge handbook of language and humor* (pp. 234–49). Routledge.

Colston, H. L., & Gibbs, R. W. (2002). Are irony and metaphor understood differently? *Metaphor and Symbol, 17*(1), 57–80. https://doi.org/10.1207/S15327868MS1701_5.

Colston, H. L., & Gibbs, R. W. (2021). Figurative language communicates directly because it precisely demonstrates what we mean. *Canadian Journal of Experimental Psychology/Revue Canadienne de Psychologie Expérimentale, 75*(2), 228–33. https://doi.org/10.1037/cep0000254.

Cornejol, C., Simonetti, F., Aldunate, N. et al. (2007). Electrophysiological evidence of different interpretative strategies in irony comprehension. *Journal of Psycholinguistic Research, 36*(6), 411–30. https://doi.org/10.1007/s10936-007-9052-0.

Cowan, N. (2005). *Working memory capacity.* Psychology Press.

Delogu, F., Brouwer, H., & Crocker, M. W. (2019). Event-related potentials index lexical retrieval (N400) and integration (P600) during language comprehension. *Brain and Cognition, 135*, 103569. https://doi.org/10.1016/j.bandc.2019.05.007.

Eviatar, Z., & Just, M. A. (2006). Brain correlates of discourse processing: An fMRI investigation of irony and conventional metaphor comprehension. *Neuropsychologia, 44*(12), 2348–59. https://doi.org/10.1016/j.neuropsychologia.2006.05.007.

Fein, O., Yeari, M., & Giora, R. (2015). On the priority of salience-based interpretations: The case of sarcastic irony. *Intercultural Pragmatics, 12*(1), 1–32. https://doi.org/10.1515/ip-2015-0001.

Ferreira, F., & Yang, Z. (2019). The problem of comprehension in psycholinguistics. *Discourse Processes, 56*(7), 485–95. https://doi.org/10.1080/0163853X.2019.1591885.

Filik, R., Howman, H., Ralph-Nearman, C., & Giora, R. (2018). The role of defaultness and personality factors in sarcasm interpretation: Evidence from eye-tracking during reading. *Metaphor and Symbol, 33*(3), 148–62. https://doi.org/10.1080/10926488.2018.1481258.

Filik, R., Ingram, J., Moxey, L., & Leuthold, H. (2021). Irony as a test of the presupposition-denial account: An ERP study. *Journal of Psycholinguistic Research, 50*(6), 1321–35. https://doi.org/10.1007/s10936-021-09795-y.

Filik, R., Leuthold, H., Wallington, K., & Page, J. (2014). Testing theories of irony processing using eye-tracking and ERPs. *Journal of Experimental Psychology: Learning, Memory, and Cognition, 40*(3), 811–28. https://doi.org/10.1037/a0035658.

Filik, R., & Moxey, L. M. (2010). The on-line processing of written irony. *Cognition, 116*(3), 421–36. https://doi.org/10.1016/j.cognition.2010.06.005.

Filik, R., Țurcan, A., Ralph-Nearman, C., & Pitiot, A. (2019). What is the difference between irony and sarcasm? An fMRI study. *Cortex, 115*, 112–22. https://doi.org/10.1016/j.cortex.2019.01.025.

Frith, C., & Frith, U. (2005). Theory of mind. *Current Biology, 15*(17), R644–R645. https://doi.org/10.1016/j.cub.2005.08.041.

Gallagher, H. L., & Frith, C. D. (2003). Functional imaging of "theory of mind." *Trends in Cognitive Sciences, 7*(2), 77–83. https://doi.org/10.1016/S1364-6613(02)00025-6.

Garmendia, J. (2014). The clash: Humor and critical attitude in verbal irony. *HUMOR, 27*(4), 641–59. https://doi.org/10.1515/humor-2014-0094.

Gibbs, R. W. (1984). Literal meaning and psychological theory. *Cognitive Science, 8*, 275–304.

Gibbs, R. W. (1986a). Comprehension and memory for nonliteral utterances: The problem of sarcastic indirect requests. *Acta Psychologica, 62*(1), 41–57. https://doi.org/10.1016/0001-6918(86)90004-1.

Gibbs, R. W. (1986b). On the psycholinguistics of sarcasm. *Journal of Experimental Psychology: General, 115*(1), 3–15. https://doi.org/10.1037/0096-3445.115.1.3.

Gibbs, R. W. (1994). *The poetics of mind: Figurative thought, language, and understanding.* Cambridge University Press.

Gibbs, R. W. (2002). A new look at literal meaning in understanding what is said and implicated. *Journal of Pragmatics, 34*, 457–86.

Gibbs, R. W. (2005). Literal and nonliteral meanings are corrupt ideas: A view from psycholinguistics. In S. Coulson & B. Lewandowska-Tomaszczyk (Eds.), *The literal and nonliteral in language and thought* (pp. 221–38). Peter Lang.

Gibbs, R. W., & Colston, H. L. (Eds.). (2007). *Irony in language and thought: A cognitive science reader.* Lawrence Erlbaum Associates.

Gibbs, R. W., & Colston, H. L. (2012). *Interpreting figurative meaning.* Cambridge University Press.

Gibbs, R. W., & Colston, H. L. (2020). Pragmatics always matters: An expanded vision of experimental pragmatics. *Frontiers in Psychology, 11,* 1619. https://doi.org/10.3389/fpsyg.2020.01619.

Giora, R. (1995). On irony and negation. *Discourse Processes, 19,* 239–64.

Giora, R. (1997). Understanding figurative and literal language: The graded salience hypothesis. *Cognitive Linguistics, 8*(3), 183–206.

Giora, R. (2002). Literal vs. Figurative language: Different or equal. *Journal of Pragmatics, 34,* 487–506.

Giora, R. (2003). *On our mind: Salience, context, and figurative language.* Oxford University Press.

Giora, R. (2021). The creativity of negation. In X. Wen & J. R. Taylor (Eds.), *The Routledge Handbook of Cognitive Linguistics* (1st ed., pp. 127–41). Routledge. https://doi.org/10.4324/9781351034708-9.

Giora, R., Drucker, A., Fein, O., & Mendelson, I. (2015). Default sarcastic interpretations: On the priority of nonsalient interpretations. *Discourse Processes, 52*(3), 173–200. https://doi.org/10.1080/0163853X.2014.954951.

Giora, R., & Fein, O. (1999). Irony: Context and salience. *Metaphor and Symbol, 14*(4), 241–57.

Giora, R., Fein, O., Laadan, D. et al. (2007). Expecting irony: Context versus salience-based effects. *Metaphor and Symbol, 22*(2), 119–46.

Giora, R., Fein, O., & Schwartz, T. (1998). Irony: Graded salience and indirect negation. *Metaphor and Symbol, 13*(2), 83–101.

Giora, R., Givoni, S., & Fein, O. (2015). Defaultness reigns: The case of sarcasm. *Metaphor and Symbol, 30*(4), 290–313. https://doi.org/10.1080/10926488.2015.1074804.

Giora, R., Jaffe, I., Becker, I., & Fein, O. (2018). Strongly attenuating highly positive concepts: The case of default sarcastic interpretations. *Review of Cognitive Linguistics, 16*(1), 19–47. https://doi.org/10.1075/rcl.00002.gio.

Giora, R., Livnat, E., Fein, O. et al. (2013). Negation generates nonliteral interpretations by default. *Metaphor and Symbol, 28*(2), 89–115. https://doi.org/10.1080/10926488.2013.768510.

Giora, R., Raphaely, M., Fein, O., & Livnat, E. (2014). Resonating with contextually inappropriate interpretations in production: The case of irony. *Cognitive Linguistics, 25*(3), 443–55. https://doi.org/10.1515/cog-2014-0026.

Glenwright, M., & Pexman, P. M. (2010). Development of children's ability to distinguish sarcasm and verbal irony. *Journal of Child Language, 37*(2), 429–51. https://doi.org/10.1017/S0305000909009520.

Grice, P. (1975). Logic and conversation. In P. Cole, J. L. Morgan, & J. P. Kimball (Eds.), *Syntax and semantics 3: Speech acts* (pp. 41–58). Academic Press.

Grice, P. (1978). Some further notes on logic and conversation. In P. Cole (Ed.), *Syntax and Semantics 9: Pragmatics* (Vol. 9, pp.113–27). Academic Press.

Grice, P. (1989). *Studies in the way of words*. Harvard University Press.

Heredia, R. R., & Cieślicka, A. B. (2015). *Bilingual figurative language processing*. Cambridge University Press.

Ivanko, S. L., Pexman, P. M., & Olineck, K. M. (2004). How sarcastic are you?: Individual differences and verbal irony. *Journal of Language and Social Psychology, 23*(3), 244–71. https://doi.org/10.1177/0261927X04266809.

Kaakinen, J. K., Olkoniemi, H., Kinnari, T., & Hyönä, J. (2014). Processing of written irony: An eye movement study. *Discourse Processes, 51*(4), 287–311. https://doi.org/10.1080/0163853X.2013.870024.

Katz, A. (2005). Discourse and sociocultural factors in understanding nonliteral language. In H. L. Colston & A. Katz (Eds.), *Figurative language comprehension: Social and cultural influences* (pp. 183–207). Routledge.

Katz, A. (2017). Chapter 11. The standard experimental approach to the study of irony: Let us not be hasty in throwing out the baby with the bathwater. In A. Athanasiadou & H. L. Colston (Eds.), *Figurative Thought and Language* (Vol. 1, pp. 237–54). John Benjamins. https://doi.org/10.1075/ftl.1.12kat.

Katz, A., Blasko, D. G., & Kazmerski, V. A. (2004). Saying what you don't mean: Social influences on sarcastic language processing. *Current Directions in Psychological Science, 13*(5), 186–89. https://doi.org/10.1111/j.0963-7214.2004.00304.x.

Katz, A., & Pexman, P. M. (1997). Interpreting figurative statements: Speaker occupation can change metaphor to irony. *Metaphor and Symbol, 12*(1), 19–41. https://doi.org/10.1207/s15327868ms1201_3.

Katz, A., & Reid, N. J. (2020). Tests of conceptual metaphor theory with episodic memory tests. *Cognitive Semantics, 6*(1), 56–82. https://doi.org/10.1163/23526416-00601003.

Kendeou, P., & O'Brien, E. J. (2018). Reading comprehension theories: A view from the top down. In M. F. Schober, D. N. Rapp, & M. A. Britt (Eds.), *The Routledge handbook of discourse processes* (2nd ed., pp. 7–21). Routledge

Kowatch, K., Whalen, J. M., & Pexman, P. M. (2013). Irony comprehension in action: A new test of processing for verbal irony. *Discourse Processes, 50*(5), 301–15. https://doi.org/10.1080/0163853X.2013.799934.

Kreuz, R. J. (2020). *Irony and sarcasm*. The MIT Press.

Kumon-Nakamura, S., Glucksberg, S., & Brown, M. (1995). How about another piece of pie: The allusional pretense theory of discourse irony. *Journal of Experimental Psychology: General, 124*(1), 3–21.

Kutas, M., & Federmeier, K. D. (2011). Thirty years and counting: Finding meaning in the N400 component of the event-related brain potential (ERP).

Annual Review of Psychology, 62(1), 621–47. https://doi.org/10.1146/annurev.psych.093008.131123.

Kutas, M., Van Petten, C. K., & Kluender, R. (2006). Psycholinguistics Electrified II (1994–2005). In *Handbook of psycholinguistics* (pp. 659–724). Elsevier. https://doi.org/10.1016/B978-012369374-7/50018-3.

Li, S., Gu, W., Liu, L., & Tang, P. (2020). The role of voice quality in Mandarin sarcastic speech: An acoustic and electroglottographic study. *Journal of Speech, Language, and Hearing Research, 63*(8), 2578–88. https://doi.org/10.1044/2020_JSLHR-19-00166.

Lœvenbruck, H., Jannet, M. A. B., D'Imperio, M., Spini, M., & Champagne-Lavau, M. (2013). Prosodic cues of sarcastic speech in French: Slower, higher, wider. *Interspeech 2013*, 3537–41. https://doi.org/10.21437/Interspeech.2013-761.

Lucariello, J. (1994). Situational irony: A concept of events gone awry. *Journal of Experimental Psychology: General, 123*(2), 129–45.

Matsui, T., Nakamura, T., Utsumi, A. et al. (2016). The role of prosody and context in sarcasm comprehension: Behavioral and fMRI evidence. *Neuropsychologia, 87*, 74–84. https://doi.org/10.1016/j.neuropsychologia.2016.04.031.

Mauchand, M., Caballero, J. A., Jiang, X., & Pell, M. D. (2021). Immediate online use of prosody reveals the ironic intentions of a speaker: Neurophysiological evidence. *Cognitive, Affective, & Behavioral Neuroscience, 21*(1), 74–92. https://doi.org/10.3758/s13415-020-00849-7.

Mauchand, M., Vergis, N., & Pell, M. (2018). Ironic tones of voices. *Speech Prosody 2018*, 443–47. https://doi.org/10.21437/SpeechProsody.2018-90.

McNamara, D. S., & Magliano, J. (2009). Toward a comprehensive model of comprehension. In *Psychology of learning and motivation* (Vol. 51, pp. 297–384). Elsevier. https://doi.org/10.1016/S0079-7421(09)51009-2.

Noveck, I. (2018). *Experimental pragmatics: The making of a cognitive science* (1st ed.). Cambridge University Press. https://doi.org/10.1017/9781316027073.

Obert, A., Gierski, F., Calmus, A. et al. (2016). Neural correlates of contrast and humor: Processing common features of verbal irony. *PLOS ONE, 11*(11), e0166704. https://doi.org/10.1371/journal.pone.0166704.

Olkoniemi, H., Johander, E., & Kaakinen, J. K. (2018). The role of look-backs in the processing of written sarcasm. *Memory & Cognition, 47*, 87–105. https://doi.org/10.3758/s13421-018-0852-2.

Olkoniemi, H., & Kaakinen, J. K. (2021). Processing of irony in text: A systematic review of eye-tracking studies. *Canadian Journal of Experimental Psychology/Revue Canadienne de Psychologie Expérimentale, 75*(2), 99–106. https://doi.org/10.1037/cep0000216

Olkoniemi, H., Ranta, H., & Kaakinen, J. K. (2016). Individual differences in the processing of written sarcasm and metaphor: Evidence from eye movements. *Journal of Experimental Psychology: Learning, Memory, and Cognition, 42*(3), 433–50. https://doi.org/10.1037/xlm0000176.

Olkoniemi, H., Strömberg, V., & Kaakinen, J. K. (2019). The ability to recognise emotions predicts the time-course of sarcasm processing: Evidence from eye movements. *Quarterly Journal of Experimental Psychology, 72*(5), 1212–23. https://doi.org/10.1177/1747021818807864.

Oxford English Dictionary. (2022). Irony, n. In *Oxford English Dictionary*.

Pexman, P. M. (2005). Social factors in the interpretation of verbal irony: The roles of speaker and listener characteristics. In H. L. Colston & A. Katz (Eds.), *Figurative language comprehension: Social and cultural influences* (pp. 209–32). Routledge.

Pexman, P. M. (2008). It's fascinating research: The cognition of verbal irony. *Current Directions in Psychological Science, 17*(4), 286–90. https://doi.org/10.1111/j.1467-8721.2008.00591.x.

Pexman, P. M., Ferretti, T. R., & Katz, A. (2000). Discourse factors that influence online reading of metaphor and irony. *Discourse Processes, 29*(3), 201–22.

Pfaff, K. L., & Gibbs, R. W. (1997). Authorial intentions in understanding satirical texts. *Poetics, 25*, 45–70. https://doi.org/10.1016/S0304-422X(97)00006-5.

Regel, S., Coulson, S., & Gunter, T. C. (2010). The communicative style of a speaker can affect language comprehension? ERP evidence from the comprehension of irony. *Brain Research, 1311*, 121–35. https://doi.org/10.1016/j.brainres.2009.10.077.

Regel, S., Gunter, T., & Friederici, A. D. (2011). Isn't it ironic? An electrophysiological exploration of figurative language processing. *Journal of Cognitive Neuroscience, 23*(2), 277–93.

Rivière, E., Klein, M., & Champagne-Lavau, M. (2018). Using context and prosody in irony understanding: Variability amongst individuals. *Journal of Pragmatics, 138*, 165–72. https://doi.org/10.1016/j.pragma.2018.10.006.

Roberts, M. (2014). *What everybody gets wrong about Alanis Morissette's "Ironic."* Salon. www.salon.com/2014/05/08/what_everybody_gets_wrong_about_alanis_morissettes_ironic_partner/.

Rothermich, K., & Pell, M. D. (2015). Introducing RISC: A new video inventory for testing social perception. *PLOS ONE, 10*(7), e0133902. https://doi.org/10.1371/journal.pone.0133902.

Rothermich, K., Schoen Simmons, E., Rao Makarla, P. et al. (2021). Tracking nonliteral language processing using audiovisual scenarios. *Canadian*

Journal of Experimental Psychology/Revue Canadienne de Psychologie Expérimentale, *75*(2), 211–20. https://doi.org/10.1037/cep0000223.

Schwoebel, J., Dews, S., Winner, E., & Srinivas, K. (2000). Obligatory processing of the literal meaning of ironic utterances: Further evidence. *Metaphor and Symbol*, *15*(1–2), 47–61.

Shelley, C. (2001). The bicoherence theory of situational irony. *Cognitive Science*, *25*(5), 775–818. https://doi.org/10.1207/s15516709cog2505_7.

Simpson, P. (2003). *On the discourse of satire: Towards a stylistic model of satirical humour.* John Benjamins.

Skalicky, S. (2019). Investigating satirical discourse processing and comprehension: The role of cognitive, demographic, and pragmatic features. *Language and Cognition*, *11*, 499–525. https://doi.org/10.1017/langcog.2019.30.

Skalicky, S. (2020). Exploring perceptions of novelty and mirth in elicited figurative language production. *Metaphor and Symbol*, *35*(2), 77–96. https://doi.org/10.1080/10926488.2020.1820763.

Skalicky, S. (In press). Modeling satirical uptake using discourse processing methods. *Discourse Processes*. https://doi.org/10.1080/0163853X.2022.2128182

Skalicky, S. (2022, July). *Recognising satirical intent in satirical news discourse: Effects of reading behaviour and need for cognition* [Standard Presentation]. 2022 Annual Meeting of the Society for Text and Discourse, Virtual Conference. https://osf.io/e8qj7/?view_only=8673be1971cb4886801e55f5a4c693ab.

Skalicky, S., & Crossley, S. A. (2019). Examining the online processing of satirical newspaper headlines. *Discourse Processes*, *56*(1), 61–76. https://doi.org/10.1080/0163853X.2017.1368332.

Sperber, D., & Wilson, D. (1981). Irony and the use mention distinction. In P. Cole (Ed.), *Radical Pragmatics* (pp. 295–318). Elsevier

Spotorno, N., Cheylus, A., Van Der Henst, J.-B., & Noveck, I. A. (2013). What's behind a P600? Integration operations during irony processing. *PLoS ONE*, *8*(6), e66839. https://doi.org/10.1371/journal.pone.0066839.

Spotorno, N., Koun, E., Prado, J., Van Der Henst, J.-B., & Noveck, I. A. (2012). Neural evidence that utterance-processing entails mentalizing: The case of irony. *NeuroImage*, *63*(1), 25–39. https://doi.org/10.1016/j.neuroimage.2012.06.046.

Spotorno, N., & Noveck, I. A. (2014). When is irony effortful? *Journal of Experimental Psychology: General*, *143*(4), 1649–65. https://doi.org/10.1037/a0036630.

Thompson, D., Leuthold, H., & Filik, R. (2021). Examining the influence of perspective and prosody on expected emotional responses to irony: Evidence from event-related brain potentials. *Canadian Journal of Experimental*

Psychology/Revue Canadienne de Psychologie Expérimentale, 75(2), 107–13. https://doi.org/10.1037/cep0000249.

Ţurcan, A., & Filik, R. (2016). An eye-tracking investigation of written sarcasm comprehension: The roles of familiarity and context. *Journal of Experimental Psychology: Learning, Memory, and Cognition, 42*(12), 1867–93. https://doi.org/10.1037/xlm0000285.

Ţurcan, A., & Filik, R. (2017). Chapter 12. Investigating sarcasm comprehension using eye-tracking during reading: What are the roles of literality, familiarity, and echoic mention? In A. Athanasiadou & H. L. Colston (Eds.), *Figurative Thought and Language* (Vol. 1, pp. 255–76). John Benjamins. https://doi.org/10.1075/ftl.1.13tuc.

Uchiyama, H., Saito, D. N., Tanabe, H. C. et al. (2012). Distinction between the literal and intended meanings of sentences: A functional magnetic resonance imaging study of metaphor and sarcasm. *Cortex, 48*(5), 563–83. https://doi .org/10.1016/j.cortex.2011.01.004.

Uchiyama, H., Seki, A., Kageyama, H. et al. (2006). Neural substrates of sarcasm: A functional magnetic-resonance imaging study. *Brain Research, 1124*(1), 100–10. https://doi.org/10.1016/j.brainres.2006.09.088.

Utsumi, A. (2000). Verbal irony as implicit display of ironic environment: Distinguishing ironic utterances from nonirony. *Journal of Pragmatics, 32,* 1777–806.

Voyer, D., & Techentin, C. (2010). Subjective auditory features of sarcasm. *Metaphor and Symbol, 25*(4), 227–42. https://doi.org/10.1080/10926488 .2010.510927.

Weissman, B., & Tanner, D. (2018). A strong wink between verbal and emoji-based irony: How the brain processes ironic emojis during language comprehension. *PLOS ONE, 13*(8), e0201727. https://doi.org/10.1371/ journal.pone.0201727.

Wikipedia. (2022). *Ironic (song)*. Wikipedia: The Free Encyclopedia. https://en .wikipedia.org/wiki/Ironic_(song).

Wilson, D., & Sperber, D. (1992). On verbal irony. *Lingua, 87*(1), 53–76.

Cambridge Elements ⹀

Psycholinguistics

Paul Warren
Victoria University of Wellington

Paul Warren is Professor of Linguistics at Victoria University of Wellington, where his teaching and research is in psycholinguistics, phonetics, and laboratory phonology. His publications include *Introducing Psycholinguistics* (2012) and *Uptalk* (2016), both published by CUP. He is a founding member of the Association for Laboratory Phonology, and a member of the Australasian Speech Science Technology Association and the International Phonetic Association. Paul is a member of the editorial boards for *Laboratory Phonology* and the *Journal of the International Phonetic Association*, and for twenty years (2000–2019) served on the editorial board of *Language and Speech*.

Advisory Board

About the Series

This Elements series presents theoretical and empirical studies in the interdisciplinary field of psycholinguistics. Topics include issues in the mental representation and processing of language in production and comprehension, and the relationship of psycholinguistics to other fields of research. Each Element is a high quality and up-to-date scholarly work in a compact, accessible format.

Cambridge Elements ≡

Psycholinguistics

Elements in the Series

Verbal Irony Processing
Stephen Skalicky

A full series listing is available at: www.cambridge.org/EPSL

Printed in the United States
by Baker & Taylor Publisher Services